CGFM

Examination 2: Governmental Accounting, Financial Reporting and Budgeting Exam

SECRETS

Study Guide
Your Key to Exam Success

CGFM Exam Review for the
Certified Government Financial
Manager Exam

Dear Future Exam Success Story:

Congratulations on your purchase of our study guide. Our goal in writing our study guide was to cover the content on the test, as well as provide insight into typical test taking mistakes and how to overcome them.

Standardized tests are a key component of being successful, which only increases the importance of doing well in the high-pressure high-stakes environment of test day. How well you do on this test will have a significant impact on your future, and we have the research and practical advice to help you execute on test day.

The product you're reading now is designed to exploit weaknesses in the test itself, and help you avoid the most common errors test takers frequently make.

How to use this study guide

We don't want to waste your time. Our study guide is fast-paced and fluff-free. We suggest going through it a number of times, as repetition is an important part of learning new information and concepts.

First, read through the study guide completely to get a feel for the content and organization. Read the general success strategies first, and then proceed to the content sections. Each tip has been carefully selected for its effectiveness.

Second, read through the study guide again, and take notes in the margins and highlight those sections where you may have a particular weakness.

Finally, bring the manual with you on test day and study it before the exam begins.

Your success is our success

We would be delighted to hear about your success. Send us an email and tell us your story. Thanks for your business and we wish you continued success.

Sincerely,

Mometrix Test Preparation Team

Need more help? Check out our flashcards at: http://MometrixFlashcards.com/CGFM

TABLE OF CONTENTS

Top 20 Test Taking Tips

1. Carefully follow all the test registration procedures
2. Know the test directions, duration, topics, question types, how many questions
3. Setup a flexible study schedule at least 3-4 weeks before test day
4. Study during the time of day you are most alert, relaxed, and stress free
5. Maximize your learning style; visual learner use visual study aids, auditory learner use auditory study aids
6. Focus on your weakest knowledge base
7. Find a study partner to review with and help clarify questions
8. Practice, practice, practice
9. Get a good night's sleep; don't try to cram the night before the test
10. Eat a well balanced meal
11. Know the exact physical location of the testing site; drive the route to the site prior to test day
12. Bring a set of ear plugs; the testing center could be noisy
13. Wear comfortable, loose fitting, layered clothing to the testing center; prepare for it to be either cold or hot during the test
14. Bring at least 2 current forms of ID to the testing center
15. Arrive to the test early; be prepared to wait and be patient
16. Eliminate the obviously wrong answer choices, then guess the first remaining choice
17. Pace yourself; don't rush, but keep working and move on if you get stuck
18. Maintain a positive attitude even if the test is going poorly
19. Keep your first answer unless you are positive it is wrong
20. Check your work, don't make a careless mistake

General Knowledge of Governmental Financial Accounting, Reporting and Budgeting

Publicly-held firms vs. government agencies

In the public sector, businesses which raise capital through the sale of stock issues are publicly owned by shareholders. The primary goal of these organizations is to improve shareholder wealth. They are accountable to those shareholders and are required to report their annual financial statements.

A government agency is a non-profit organization established to protect the public and/or to encourage social and economic development. They are funded by taxpayer dollars, which obligates them to follow more stringent laws regarding their appropriation of funds. They are required to provide a description of the programs they offer, establish a budget, and maintain a system for ensuring all expenditures stay within the budget.

Business-type vs. governmental activities

Business-type activities of state and local governments are those in which the government offers a product or service in exchange for a fee, such as charging admission to a city pool. Typically cash inflows of business-type activities match their cash outflows. For example admission fees are correlated to a service's operating expense, and a product price is correlated to the cost of its production. Business-type activities are recorded using the accrual method of accounting.

The cash inflows and outflows of governmental activities, however, are mismatched. The majority of revenues come from taxes collected and grants received, yet the outflow of funds is disbursed among many projects, programs, and services. Thus no direct link exists between revenues and expenditures. Therefore, a modified accrual method of accounting is used to record governmental activities. Using this method, revenues are deferred until they become useable and measurable, at which time, they are recognized and recorded; expenditures are only recognized and recorded when they are paid with current assets; and immaterial prepaid expenses are expensed at the time of payment.

Accountability

The types of accountability associated with a government agency are as follows:
- *Legal Accountability* refers to the requirement for government agencies to abide by applicable laws and regulations.
- *Performance Accountability* refers to the need for authoritative figures of a government agency to effectively pursue the achievement of the agency's objectives.
- *Fiscal Accountability* refers to the duty of a government agency's key leaders to report the agency's sources of funding and other resources, as well as, its distribution of resources and expenditures.
- *Operational Accountability* refers to a government agency's need to prove that it is meeting its obligation to protect or improve society. This may be accomplished by reporting performance measures.

Financial reports from government agencies are used to hold the agencies accountable for the way public funds are spent. They are a means for ensuring the funds are spent appropriately, within a predetermined budget, and in accordance with laws and regulations. They are useful in determining if unfavorable financial situations are due to internal causes, such as misallocation of funds, or are due to external causes, such as a recession, or a bit of both. They also assist officials in making decisions related to an agency's programs and objectives.

Reports

Government financial reports and performance reports are used by:
- *Legislators*: They review the reports to ensure expenditures are appropriate and abide by budgetary and legal guidelines.
- *Investors:* They study them to assess the financial soundness of investing in particular government debt securities.
- *The General Public*: They are interested in understanding how their tax money is being spent. Also the documentation is a means by which to hold their government officials accountable.
- *Creditors*: They check the reports to verify the funds borrowed from them are being spent in ways the government promised.

The three main areas on a financial report that users utilize to assess a government agency:
- *Resources*: They view the descriptions of funding sources or other resources.
- *Resource Allocation*: They read the explanation of where resources are being used. This is important for determining if resources are being used efficiently and may help assess whether the program's purpose is still valid.

- *Budgets:* They look over the proposed spending limits within areas of the government agency. Users of government financial reports review budgets to assess the appropriateness of spending allocations and to ensure they fit within legal and regulatory requirements.

Different types of financial reports include:
- *Point-in-time Reports*: Also known as stock reports, reveal an entity's financial state as of a particular date in time, which is typically the report's date.
- *Period Reports*: Show an entity's revenues and expenses during a period of time, usually a fiscal year.
- *General Purpose External Financial Reports (GPEFR)*: Refers to externally audited financial statements, accompanied by notes of explanation or extra provided information in response to any auditor questions or concerns.

For effective communication of financial information, governmental financial reports should be:
- *Understandable:* They should have information organized so that anyone with a background in government accounting may interpret them with ease.
- *Reliable*: In order for the information to be reliable, it must be true, consistent, and correct.
- *Relevant:* To be relevant, a financial report must be completed in a timely fashion so that it contains current information.
- *Timely*: Not only should financial reports be produced in a timely fashion, they must also be distributed to their users within a reasonable time period so they are useful to decision-makers.
- *Consistent*: The same accounting methods must be applied for each time period. Should a change in accounting methods become necessary, full disclosure of the reasons for the change, as well as, an explanation of the effects the change has had on the report must accompany that report.
- *Comparability*: Governmental financial reports should be organized in a similar fashion so that reports from various government agencies may be compared.

The Reports Consolidation Act of 2000

The purpose of the Reports Consolidation Act of 2000 is to consolidate the financial management report and the annual performance reports into one report, known as the Performance and Accountability report. It requires agencies to coordinate information, making the process more efficient, as well as, producing a higher-quality, more useful report for the President, Congress, and the general public to review.

Due process

In proposing a revised or new accounting or reporting standard to the Government Accounting Standards Board (GASB), (GASB) allows individuals or organizations to propose projects that re-evaluate current accounting or reporting standards, as well as, ones that establish the need for new standards. This action requires following a due process. After the required research is given to GASB, the Board consults with the Governmental Accounting Standards Advisory Council (GASAC) on whether the project should be added to the agenda for further consideration, placed on hold, or dismissed. If it is added to the current agenda, the GASB Chairman assigns the project a task force of 15-25 members, which provide a fair geographical and constituent representation. Once a project reaches the phase of proposing new or alternative standards, the Board votes on which document the project members may use to do so: a discussion memorandum, an invitation to comment, a preliminary review, or an exposure draft.

The following documents may be used during due process:
- A *discussion memorandum*: May be the first document a project uses to suggest alternative accounting or reporting methods. This serves as an opening for a discussion of ideas and issues surrounding the proposals.
- An *invitation to comment*: The document typically selected by the Board to be used when there is controversy surrounding the issues of concern.
- A *preliminary views document*: Explains the Board's preliminary view, including any alternative views supported by at least two Board members.
- An *exposure draft*: Documentation of the Board's proposal to the public regarding a new or revised standard. It takes into account all relevant research, opinions from the project's task force and the GASAC, and other public responses. This is the last stage of the due process. Proposals that make it this far usually become a final standard.

Responses, mailed or emailed, to all due process documents are collected for 30 - 120 days from the date the document is issued.

Measurement focus

A measurement focus determines how a transaction is measured, recognized, and recorded. The *economic resources* measurement focus considers the economic impact of a transaction when determining how to measure and record it. This focus ensures revenues are matched to expenses when they are incurred. It capitalizes fixed assts (i.e., plant and equipment) and depreciates them over their useful life. Accrued interest on long-term debt is expensed on the operating statement, and liability is reduced when payments on principal are made.

The *current financial resources* measurement focus is strictly concerned with the entity's liquidity, meaning cash, other liquid assets, and short-term debt. Its goal is to ensure there are enough revenues to cover short-term debts.

Example: Based on the *economic resources measurement focus*, the purchase of a $2000 copy machine would have no immediate economic impact on the government; a copy machine worth $2000 is equivalent to $2000 in cash. However the copy machine may have a useful life of only 10 years. As the copy machine gets older, its value is depleted; this does have an economic impact on the government's financial condition. Therefore, each year the asset value would be reduced by $200 ($2000 / 10years useful life) and recorded as a depreciation expense.

The purchase of the copy machine under the *current financial resources measurement* focus would be viewed as giving up $2000 of a current asset (cash) in exchange for a $2000 long-term asset (the copy machine). Therefore it would be recorded as a $2000 expenditure on the operating statement, and no further entries would be needed.

Converting measurement focus
Capital purchases within a governmental fund, which are recorded using the current financial resources measurement, are shown as expenses. However, when they are to be reported on the government-wide operating statement, they must be reported using the economic resources measurement focus. Therefore adjusting entries must be made to convert the measurement focus so that capital purchases are reported as assets and only a year's depreciation is expensed. To make this conversion, the Capital Asset account is debited while the Capital Outlay account is credited for the same amount.

Outstanding bonds are also reported differently by the two measurement focuses, and therefore require adjusting entries. Bonds, measured by the current financial resources focus, are recorded as a cash inflow. According to the economic resources focus, however, they must be converted to long-term debt. This is done by debiting the Other Financing Sources account and crediting the Long-term Debt account for the same amount.

Standards and Legislation

FASAB
The purpose of the Federal Accounting Standards Advisory Board (FASAB) is to create accounting standards for federal agencies to follow as they account for transactions and prepare their required annual financial statements. To establish useful standards, the FASAB first determines who the statements' primary users are and what needs they have. Anticipated costs and benefits are considered before a standard is implemented, and a standard's effects are studied after it has been implemented. The FASAB's objective is to develop accounting standards that provide consistency among the agencies' accounting practices, maintain

objectiveness in the reporting, and improve the understanding and usability of the financial reports.

Generally Accepted Accounting Principles
According to the Statement of Auditing Standards No. 69, Generally Accepted Accounting Principles (GAAP) for state and local governments are classified into the following categories:

- *Category A:* This grouping consists of accounting principles that have been formally established. Statements and interpretations directed toward state and local governments issued by the GASB, AICPA, and FASB are included in this category.
- *Category B:* This grouping consists of Technical Bulletins regarding state and local governments that have been issued by GASB and AICPA.
- *Category C:* This category's objective is to have a consensus reached on accounting matters. It includes the accounting principles of the AICPA Accounting Standards Executive Committee.
- *Category D:* This grouping contains GASB's question-and-answer guides on how to implement accounting methods and standards.

GASB
The purpose of the Government Accounting Standards Board (GASB) is to develop effective accounting methods and to maintain a consistency in the financial reporting of all state and local governments. The non-profit, private organization accomplishes these goals by conducting research in its continuous quest for improved accounting techniques. Successful findings are posted as generally accepted accounting principles (GAAP) for state and local governments to adopt. Financial reporting standards determined by GASB are meant for external financial reports, not internal reports. Users of the external financial reports, according to the GASB are: general public, members of Congress, the media, interest groups, investors, and creditors.

The **GASB Statement 34** views the government as one whole entity as it expresses the expectation for the government to keep public revenues/resources safe until they are needed, as well as, to ensure that revenues are used in ways that comply with stipulated rules, laws, and regulations. The purpose of the statement is to promote accountability among government officials over operations involving revenues, finances, and budgets, as well as, compliance with applicable laws.

The GASB **Concepts Statement 1** specifies the main objectives of financial reporting that should be met as:

- Adequately conveying the government's efforts and accomplishments.
- Supplying adequate information regarding the acquisition and expenditure of revenues/resources.
- Disclosing all legal and contractual limitations on revenues/resources.

- Ensuring legal compliance on the government's behalf while handling revenues/resources.
- Allowing users to determine the government's level of accountability.
- Reporting sufficient information which shows how financial obligations were met and the year's overall operating results.
- Providing sufficient information so users are able to determine the government's current financial position in relation to previous years.

Accountability of Tax Dollars Act

The Accountability of Tax Dollars Act of 2002 requires all executive branch agencies to annually prepare audited financial statements. However, the act gives the acting director of the Office of Management and Budgets the authority to exempt an agency from these requirements if: the agency has an annual budget authority of under $25 million, the agency's activities possess a low financial risk, and no concerns were raised after reviewing the agency's performance history.

OMB Circular A-11, Part 4

The OMB Circular A-11, Part 4 has "Instructions on Budget Execution". It describes apportionment as a budgeting plan that each level of government must establish. Apportionment plans show the proposed allocation of funds. They must comply with all applicable laws and require the Office of Management and Budget's approval. To develop an apportionment plan, government agencies must identify their programs. The purpose of apportionment is to oversee the use of revenues. Apportionment plans are important for ensuring that spending on government programs will be fairly balanced and that funds will be spent in a justified manner.

CFR Section 225

Certain costs incurred from administering a federal grant are eligible for reimbursement. The purpose of Section 225 in the Code of Federal Regulations (previously OMB Circular A-87) is to give state, local, and tribal governments a basis for determining which costs are eligible. It also establishes a common procedure for all government levels to follow in obtaining such reimbursement.
Guidelines for allowable costs include:
- Costs are exclusively incurred from the administration of federal grants or awards.
- Costs were determined according to generally accepted accounting principles (GAAP).
- Costs have not been previously submitted for other federal awards.
- Costs are reported with the inclusion of applicable credits.
- Costs are reasonable. Reasonableness is determined as:
  - Costs are ordinary, comparable to market prices, and necessary for running the government entity and administrating federal grants and awards.
  - Costs incurred are within the agreement terms of the grant or award, as well as, all legal and regulatory parameters.

SFFAC No. 2

The Statement of Federal Financial Accounting Concepts (SFFAC) No. 2 discusses the purpose for financial statements as being the medium through which a government agency's financial data and related information is revealed. The SFFAC No. 2 also specifies required information to be included in a government agency's financial statements. Finally, it indicates that a government agency must meet the following conditions to be deemed a reporting entity:

- The government agency has management to oversee and to be held accountable for: following and enforcing the budget, allocating resources, and producing goods and/or services.
- The government agency's financial statements provide a sufficient representation of its scope and overall financial condition for the fiscal year.

According to the SFFAC No. 2, the following information is required to be on the Balance Sheet:

- *Assets*
  - The *Fund Balance with Treasury,* showing the appropriated funds available to the government agency for designated purposes.
  - *Cash and other liquid assets*, such as checks, money orders, bank drafts, foreign currencies, deposited funds in other financial institutions, liquid assets in transit, and amounts held in imprest funds.
  - All *Security Investments*, including government and corporate securities.
  - *Receivables*, which not only include payments owed to the government from business-type activities and loans but also interest earned.
  - *Inventories and Related Properties*, showing inventory items for sale, inventory items in production, operating materials, supplies, and seized or forfeited properties.
  - *Property Plant and Equipment* which are physical assets having a useful life of greater than two years.
- *Liabilities:* This should indicate the amounts owed by the agency for goods/services already received.
- *Net Position:* This is determined by finding the difference between total assets and liabilities.

Different ways costs may be grouped on it according to the Statement of Federal Financial Accounting Concepts No. 2

According to the Statement of Federal Financial Accounting Concepts No. 2, the purpose for the Statement of Net Costs is to report accurate and dependable information about a government agency's net costs. The following information should be contained in the statement: monetary outlays, all program revenues earned, consumption of assets, manufacturing costs, delivery costs, normal operating liabilities, as well as, liabilities from business activities. The general format of the Statement of Net Costs may group costs in different ways. They may be categorized by program, sub-organization, object class, or by some combination thereof.

Government's financial information users

Users of the federal government's financial information may be classified as follows:

- *Citizens:* This is the largest classification as it includes all citizens, even those that are not taxpayers. Users in this grouping have varying degrees of interest in the financial information; those with an exceptionally strong interest would include state and local governments, the media, academics, and high-level company executives.
- *Congress:* This grouping includes not just the members of Congress but also their staff. Users that are particularly interested are members of the Congressional Budget Office, as well as, the Government Accountability Office.
- *Executives:* This grouping is made up of government leaders, such as the president, his program heads, the heads of federal agencies, as well as, their deputies and assistants. The head of the Department of Treasury, top bureau officials, and those with high positions within the Office of Management and Budgets are also part of this user classification.
- *Program Managers*: This group is comprised of federal program managers.

Administrative and internal controls

To detect and prevent significant deficiencies in the accounting and administrative policies and procedures, it is important to have a system of internal controls. Without them, our nation's finances would be at risk for a potentially devastating occurrence. The internal controls over accounting deter and detect fraudulent incidents, such as collusion and embezzlement among other illegal activities by ensuring that transactions follow all applicable laws and regulations. The administrative controls ensure transaction recordkeeping is done correctly and in a timely fashion. Since controls play a significant role in risk-reduction, the government is obligated to report information on the systems and controls used in federal financial reporting. Users of the reports may use this information to determine whether there are adequate administrative and internal controls.

Component units

Primary governments create organizations within themselves known as component units as a means for being able to submit thorough and accurate financial reports. During the establishment of a component unit, two factors must be determined:

- *Component's relationship to primary government:* It must be decided whether the component unit will remain as part of the primary government or be a legally separate entity.

- *Financial accountability:* It must be decided whether or not the component unit will be held financially accountable to the primary government. This decision will be based on the following factors:
  - o Will the number of component members that are appointed by the primary government make a voting majority?
  - o Will the primary government be allowed to make rules and regulations for the component?
  - o Will the component's financial results effect the primary government?

Factors to consider while creating a component unit which determine if the component is to be financially accountable to the primary government are:
- *Number of appointed members*: If the component's number of members appointed by the primary government makes a voting majority, the component unit is considered to be accountable to the primary government.
- *Imposition of the primary government:* If the primary government has the authority to influence the component unit's operations, the component is accountable to the primary government. The primary government's degree of influence over the component which would make it accountable would include the abilities to: hire and fire employees, remove appointed officials, veto decisions, as well as, approve, change, or reject budgets.

Inclusion in the primary government's financial reports
If the component unit does not have the authority without the primary government's consent to create and change its own budget, levy taxes, issue bonds, or determine fees; then its financial records should be included in the primary government's reports.

Blending method and the Discrete Presentation method
There are different methods for reporting a component unit's financial data in the primary government's financial statements:
- *Blending method:* This method "blends" the component unit's financial data by reporting it in the same fashion as the primary government's data.
- *Discrete Presentation method:* This method reports the component unit's financial data separately, often using columns to segregate its data from the primary government's figures, in the financial reports.

The primary government should consider the identity of the customer who purchases the component unit's offered goods or services when determining which method, Blending or Discrete Presentation, to use.

Governmental financial reporting

Assessing financial position and assessing results of operations

For many years now, the government has been required to provide the public with financial reports to ensure that the average investor could see the financial position of the country as well as those of the underlying agencies and departments that make up the federal government. This has led to the ability to invest one's money more wisely and better understand the budgetary process. However, just like with publicly traded organization, not all financial reports were created using the same underlying standards that made it difficult to do a side-by side comparison to assess operations results. This was resolved partially by implementing standards under the Generally Accepted Accounting Principles (GAAP) and the International Public Sector Accounting Standards Board (IPSAS). The idea is that by having all departments and agencies follow the same GAAP rules when preparing and reviewing financial data, the resulting statements will be more consistent.

Assessing budgetary compliance and compliance with regulations

While the process of implementing the federal budget is unique, in many ways the underlying principles echo those seen in any corporate boardroom. Each governmental agency is required to provide reports and be part of interviews where budgetary and regulatory compliance is reviewed. In addition, they must be prepared to provide feedback on how they used the funds they were given the prior year and how continuing to receive funds will better the lives of the citizens of the country. This is done through a series of meetings, governmental agency auditors, congressional hearings, and conversations with the appropriations committees each year. Based on this process, the agency may receive a smaller or larger piece of the overall pie than they did previously.

International Public Sector Accounting Standards Board

The International Public Sector Accounting Standards Board (IPSASB) is tasked with developing accounting standards that can be used as government and public-sector entities around the world are creating financial statements. The goal of the group is to increase the quality and consistency in the financial statements, regardless of the geographic location or national language of the entity. The idea is that numbers should be universal even if language is not. The group employs accountants who are associated with the International Federation of Accountants. Part of their role is to provide ongoing training with those entities who specifically request it. Approximately 130 countries are affiliated with the organization.

Requirements of open government financial reporting

Based on feedback received by the citizens of the United Sates, the federal government and the majority of state governments now use open government financial reporting. The idea behind this type of financial reporting is to provide ongoing visibility and transparency and develop trust with the public. Each year, participating governments issue a complete report as well as a guide to ensure understanding of the annual financial report. The guide allows people to have a better understanding of the components of the financial statements. Because these reports are published online, investors can review the financial statements against prior years to determine the overall direction of the government.

Comprehensive Annual Financial Report

The Comprehensive Annual Financial Report (CAFR) is a presentation that details the financial condition of the state's activities each fiscal year. The report is broken down into three parts:
1. Introductory Section: This includes a letter summarizing the results and allows the government to point out anything it would like to draw attention to.
2. Financial Section: This is the meat of the report as it includes the auditor's report, financial statements, supplementary reports, and footnotes.
3. Statistical Section: This is the section of the report that provides statistical data, including demographics.

Reporting of fund balance in governmental funds

The term *fund balance* in its simplest definition is the difference between assets and liabilities split out between reserved funds (those that cannot be moved to fund another project) and unreserved (those that are more flexible). In addition, fund balances can be broken down as follows:
1. Specific revenue funds, used to report revenue sources that are being used for a specific purpose
2. Debt service funds, used to pay outstanding debt
3. Capital projects funds, used to track the funds that will be used to acquire, build, or refurbish capital assets
4. Permanent funds, used to hold reserve funds that produce income and cannot be spent
5. General fund, used as a catch-all fund (i.e., funds that are not reported in another fund)

Accounting

Cost accounting

Cost accounting in a government entity is used to track cash flow and other financial facts which allow officials to determine if resources are being used productively and within budget. Furthermore this information is used to decide which programs are being run efficiently and which ones are not. It also helps determine which programs should be charging a fee, and what amount that fee should be. Additionally, a government agency may use the information from cost accounting to compare its performance and financial objectives with those of similar government agencies.

The federal accounting standards for cost accounting require the following of all federal agencies:
- They must use either a cost accounting system or cost finding technique, depending on the complexity of their operations, for accumulating and reporting their costs on a consistent and regular basis.
- Cost information should be gathered from managerially selected responsibility segments which have had their outputs defined.
- Outputs should have their full costs measured and reported, including the costs of contributing goods or services from other entities.
- The type of costing methodology, such as activity-based costing or job order costing, should be selected based on the entity's operating environment.
- All cost accounting procedures should be documented with instructions and exemplary forms in a manual.

Direct vs. indirect costs
Direct costs are costs directly incurred from producing a product and/or providing a service. Examples of direct costs include the cost of raw materials and employee wages.

Indirect costs, also known as overhead costs, cannot be directly associated with a particular product or service, as these types of costs contribute to several outputs or more than one service. Examples of indirect costs include rental fees for the building, electric bills, and heating bills.

When assigning costs to a product or service output, typically costs that have a direct connection to an output are assigned to that output. For costs that do not have a direct connection, they are assigned on a cause-and-effect basis. In some cases neither method applies. If that is the situation, another method may be used as long as costs are assigned reasonably and consistently.

Allocating indirect costs

When a government agency has multiple main functions, indirect costs are divided into cost groupings. Each grouping must have an indirect cost rate figured, as well as, an equitable base established. The indirect costs may then be allocated to the outputs of each function. For example, suppose an agency provides two services. Service A uses the facilities two days a week while Service B uses the facilities three days a week. The facility's rental cost must be split between the two services: Service A would be assigned 40% of the rental cost since they use it 2 out of 5 business days a week, and Service B would be assigned 60% of the rental cost since they use it 3 out of 5 business days a week. If Service B uses the facilities to produce brochures on 1 of its 3 days during the week, then 1/3 of the 60% of total facility rental cost may be assigned to the cost of brochure production.

Cost rates

The different cost rates used for different situations include:

- *Provisional Rate:* A provisional rate is established when there have been past projects of a similar nature, which may be used to *estimate* a current project's expected costs.
- *Predetermined Rate*: When there have not been any similar previous projects, a predetermined rate must be used to *estimate* a project's costs.
- *Fixed Rate*: When a sufficient amount of information allows *actual* costs and uses to be determined, a fixed rate is used.
- *Final Rate*: The *actual* costs and uses of a completed project will determine the final rate.

Fund accounting

Fund accounting simplifies having to account for the entire government by dividing it into smaller independent entities, known as funds. A government may have as many funds as deemed necessary. They are created based on an area's programs, projects, goals, and objectives. Each one is responsible for its own accounting of segregated resources and may be subject to specific regulations. This fund structure ensures a system of accountability for how revenues and resources are used and spent, as individual financial fund reports must disclose their allocation of funds. It should be noted that the entire government may not be assessed based on an individual fund report, rather all the fund reports in aggregate would be needed for such an assessment.

Accounting of governmental funds

The accounting of governmental funds is done with a current financial resources measurement focus and a modified accrual accounting basis. As a result, only current assets are recognized; cash transactions are shown on the operating statement; all monetary outflows, including those spent on capital assets or used to reduce long-term debt, are recorded as expenses; accrued interest earned or owed is not recognized until it is received or paid; revenue received from a debt issuance (i.e., bonds or notes) or from capital assets sold are classified as other financing sources; and funds that are unavailable for appropriation are reported as fund balance reservations.

Types of funds
There are three types of funds: governmental, proprietary, and fiduciary.
- *Governmental funds:* Established based on the general public service they provide. Examples include welfare programs and the police. The revenues and other resources of this type of fund typically do not equal its expenses.
- *Proprietary funds:* Require a fee for their creation. The accounting of a proprietary fund must ensure revenues match expenses.
- *Fiduciary fund:* Established in situations where the government has the role of an agent or trustee. For example, the government's employee pension fund is a fiduciary fund because the government is a trustee on the employees' behalf, and it is responsible for keeping the funds segregated from all other government activities.

Governmental funds
Types of governmental funds:
- *Special revenue funds: E*stablished based on their particular sources of revenue and are often created to pursue the interests of a politician. The politician usually has legislation passed to ensure that the fund's resources are separated from other funds and to place legal restrictions on how the fund's resources are spent. The fund's balance is reported as restricted assets on the statement of net assets.
- *Capital project funds*: Established for the purpose of financing long-term capital projects. They receive their revenues from taxes, earned interest, intergovernmental grants, and bond issues. The issuance of bonds, however, is subject to an increasing number of legal requirements, which heightens the importance for adequate internal controls over its accounting. The capital project fund's balance is reported as restricted assets on the statement of net assets.
- *Debt Service Funds*: The creation of this type of governmental fund is legally mandated by the GASB Codification Section 1300 when resources (primarily tax revenues, grants, and earned investment income) are gathered for the single purpose of paying principal and interest on bond issues. Debt service funds may also acquire resources that are transferred from other funds. Serial bonds, term bonds, and bond indentures are all types of bonds that may require a debt service fund. These funds are regulated by the GASB Codification Section 1300.
- *Agency Funds*: These are established to maintain accounting records of funds overseen by a government that is acting as a trustee or custodian. To meet the criteria of an agency fund, the government is prohibited from taking on certain administrative duties of the fund, and government programs are not allowed to receive any monetary benefit from the fund. An agency fund is

- 16 -

classified as a fiduciary fund. Employee salaries would be an example of an agency fund.

- *Permanent funds*: Set up when the government is the beneficiary of a citizen's private donation or bequest. Since the citizen usually predetermines how the funds are to be spent, the government only gets to freely use the interest earned on the donation for its own benefit. Therefore, the earned interest is siphoned out and placed in a special revenue fund where accounting records are kept of its use. Permanent funds are classified as governmental funds.
- *Private funds:* When the government is a trustee, rather than a beneficiary, of a private donation or bequest, a private-purpose fund is created instead of a permanent fund. The beneficiary is usually citizens, organizations, or other governments. An example of this arrangement would be a private-purpose fund set up for an individual's donation to a public library. If any part of the donation is invested, the investment income earned is typically restricted to specified uses. Private-purpose funds are classified as fiduciary funds.
- *Government fund:* The governmental fund is not only a major fund, but it is the most important of all governmental funds. Governments may have only one general fund, which accounts for all of the government's financial resources (except for those restricted to other funds). The general government fund, however, may have several accounts within it. Most of the fund's resources come from property taxes, sales taxes, income taxes, permit fees, and license fees; other resources include intergovernmental grants and shared revenues. The general fund may forward advances or subsidies to other funds. The recording of cash flows and account balances must follow GAAP and legal guidelines.

Operating statement for governmental funds

An operating statement reports cash flows and the beginning and ending balances of current financial resources. More specifically, it begins with revenues. Revenues are classified according to their sources, such as particular taxes (i.e., property taxes, income taxes). Next on the statement are the expenditures, which are grouped by the specific function or program they were put towards The difference between assets and liabilities is reported as excess. Then other financing resources are explained. These include revenues or resources received from debt issues, transfers, and capital leases. Any special items follow. Finally, the beginning and ending fund balances for the periods are revealed.

Balance sheets of governmental funds

The balance sheet of governmental funds should show all assets equivalent to all liabilities plus fund balances. Fund balances should be categorized as reserved or unreserved. Reserved fund balances are those that have already been committed somewhere, such as funds set aside for inventories, while unreserved fund balances are immediately available. The unreserved fund balances should be further categorized as designated and undesignated, whereby designated resources have a predetermined use. In addition to the breakdown of fund balances, current assets are also to be reported on the balance sheet of a governmental fund.

The following key points pertain to the reconciliation of the total governmental fund balance and the net assets of governmental activity:
- Capital assets, long-term liabilities, and current long-term obligations do not belong on the fund-level balance sheet. However, they do belong on the government-wide statements of net assets, along with the assets and liabilities of the internal service fund.
- Capital assets' depreciation costs are shown as historical costs.
- Revenues that are considered deferred, simply because they are not immediately available, should not be classified as deferred on the statement of net assets.

Some reconciliation items pertaining to changes in governmental funds' balances and net assets are reported on the fund-level statements, and some items belong on the government-wide statements.

Reconciling items that should be reported on the fund-level statements include:
- Resources spent on capital assets
- Revenue from capital assets sold
- Retired principal
- Deferred revenue recognized during the reporting period
- Interest paid
- Cost of bond issues, premiums, and discounts

Reconciling items that should be reported on the government-wide statements include:
- Gains and losses from capital assets sold
- Depreciation
- Changes in long-term obligations
- Revenue classified as deferred simply due to unavailability during the reporting period
- Accrued interest
- Yearly amortized expense
- The internal service fund's net revenues

Proprietary funds

The accounting of the government's business-type activities is done in *enterprise funds*. These funds are subject to the applicable requirements of FASB (those issued after November 1989) and GASB. To determine what constitutes a business-type activity, the GASB Codification Section 1300.109 has listed the following criteria:

- The activity charges a fee to sustain its existence.
- The activity has a legal obligation to use only fee-based revenues (not taxes) to pay its service and capital costs.
- Capital costs determine the price of fees charged for the service.

If an activity has even one of the above characteristics, it must be accounted for in an enterprise fund.

The accounting of goods/services offered internally within a government or to other governments is done in an *internal service fund*. Ideally, the fund's balance should be neutral, with no significant net changes. A large gain would indicate that fees for the product or service are set too high; likewise, a huge deficit would indicate that fees are set too low. Another use for internal service funds is for keeping accounting records of investments with unusually high risk levels.

Statement of Net Assets for proprietary funds

There are two approaches for preparing the Statement of Net Assets for proprietary funds. One way is similar to the fund balance sheet, whereby assets are shown to be equivalent to the sum of liabilities and equity (assets = liabilities + equity). The net assets approach shows assets minus liabilities, resulting in total net assets shown at the bottom of the column (assets – liabilities = net assets). No matter which method is used, assets and liabilities are required to be classified with long and short term assets and liabilities being reported separately. It should be noted that capital contributions are no longer included as capital assets. Also, net assets should be broken down to show invested capital assets, net of related debt; restricted assets; and unrestricted assets. Restricted assets are ones that have limitations due to outside parties (i.e., creditors and contributors).

All major funds are given their own individual column on the statement, and the smaller funds are aggregated into one single column. Any of the internal service fund's assets or liabilities that were reclassified as business-type activities should be reconciled.

Operating Statement for proprietary funds

Operating Statements for proprietary funds are detailed in that they are all-inclusive. Beginning with figures from operations, the operating statement shows: itemized operating revenues, total operating revenues, itemized operating expenses, total operating expenses, and then the resulting operating income or loss. Following that, the order of items should include: itemized and total non-operating revenues; itemized and total non-operating expenses; income before revenues/expenses, gains/losses, and transfers; capital contributions; increases to permanent or term endowments; special items; extraordinary items; transfers; increase/decrease in net assets; beginning net assets; and finally ending net assets.

Statement of Cash Flow for proprietary funds

The Statement of Cash Flows for proprietary funds should be prepared using the direct method, which means adequate details should be supplied for all cash inflows and outflows that were directly related to operating activities. Cash flows from non-capital financing activities and investment activities do not require the same detailing as those from operating activities, but they should still be included on the Statement of Cash Flows. Examples of cash inflows that are expected to be seen on the Statement of Cash Flows include: sales revenue, cash reimbursements, and cash grants received. Examples of cash outflows that should be on the Statement of Cash Flows include cash spent on: materials, employees and/or suppliers, goods, services, and taxes.

Fiduciary funds

Pension trust funds keep track of and record the government's current and future pension payments to government employees, as well as, payments relating to health and disability benefits. In this arrangement, the government serves as a trustee or agent for its employees. Separate pension trust funds are established for the different individual retirement plans. The assets of one trust fund may not be commingled with those of another. These types of funds should be established according to the Pension Guidance provided in GASB Statement Numbers 25, 26, and 27.

Investment trust funds are established, according to GASB Statement Number 31, when a government or government agency holds investment pools that are legally separate from the government. The portions of investments that are held within the government are reported as assets, and like all assets within an investment trust fund, they are reported at fair market value.

Major funds

A major fund is one in which the fund's assets, liabilities, revenues, or expenses total 10 percent or greater than the respective category for all categorical funds and fund types; and additionally, it totals 5 percent or greater than the aggregate of all funds' respective category. This 5 and 10 percent basis needs to be met by only one category (assets, liabilities, revenues, or expenses) in order for the fund to be considered major.

Interfund activities

There are two types of interfund activities:

- *Reciprocal interfund activities*: Ones involving an exchange between two funds. For example, interfund services are reciprocal. A service is provided by one fund in exchange for a fee from another fund. Also, interfund loans involve an exchange; a loan is given in exchange for loan payments. When interfund services are provided, assets and liabilities are unaffected. However, assets and liabilities are affected by interfund loans.
- *Non-reciprocal activities*: Those not involving an exchange, such as interfund transfers and interfund reimbursements. Neither one has an effect on assets and liabilities.

Interfund loans

An interfund loan is when one fund makes a loan to another fund. These types of loans affect the balance sheet or statement of net assets, but in no way do they affect the operating statement. The lender's records will show the loan as an asset due from other funds, and the recipient will show the loan as a liability due to other funds. Cash balances from internal investment pools should never be reported as negative. Therefore if a borrowing fund cannot afford the loan payments during the time it is waiting for a reimbursement, a loan from a different fund should be obtained to bring the negative balance to zero. Interfund loans must be disclosed in the notes to the financial statements.

Internal service funds

Internal service funds are established as a means for a government to be able to offer goods and services to other governmental units. The internal service fund records the payments received for its products or services as revenue. Meanwhile the governmental unit records the payments sent as an expense or expenditure.

- *Interfund Services Provided and Used:* This transaction refers to one government fund providing goods and/or services to another government fund in exchange for a payment. This type of transaction is recorded as an exchange transaction.
- *Interfund Reimbursement:* This occurs when a government fund reimburses another government fund for expenses/expenditures paid for on its behalf.
- *Interfund Transfers:* This is a transaction in which one fund transfers financing resources to another fund without any expectation of reimbursement. This type of transaction is reported as a nonreciprocal interfund activity unless the transfer involves a primary government contributing to a discrete component unit. In that case, the primary government records the transaction amount as a program expense and the component unit records it as a contribution.

Bonds

Proprietary funds and enterprise funds record the costs of a bond issue as deferred charges. The costs are deferred and amortized over the life of the bond issue. As the annual cost of the bond issue is realized, it is recorded as an expense, and deferred charges are reduced by the same amount. Governmental funds record the cost of a bond issue as an expenditure.

General Obligation Bonds versus Revenue Bonds:

- *General Obligation Bond*: This type of debt security may be repaid using various tax sources, and so repayment of the debt plus the promised interest is fully backed by the government. This makes them a safe investment. Because there is little risk to the investor, the offered interest rate is usually low. These bonds are the most popular choice among all government levels.
- *Revenue Bond*: This type of debt obligation is repaid from only the revenues earned from the operation of the financed project, such as a toll bridge. Therefore the investment is only partially backed by the government, as payment is only guaranteed to the extent that there is enough revenue generated from the project. Investors are compensated for this added risk by receiving a higher interest rate on their investment.

Types of bonds include:

- *Serial Bonds:* Bonds within a single issue that have a series of differing maturity dates. This type of financing helps the government slowly retire its debt over time.
- *Term Bonds:* A bond issue in which all the bonds mature on the same date. The government makes interest payments during the life of the bond and repays the principal on the maturity date.
- *Zero Coupon Bonds:* Instead of making periodic payments to the bondholders, the government pays all the principal and interest due on the day of maturity.

Since zero coupon and term bonds have the entire principal amount due on their maturity date, a sinking fund is set up to ensure that the government will have enough funds to retire them.

Bond Anticipation Notes

Notes are government-backed short-term debt instruments. The government repays the principle amount plus interest within one year or less. When cash flows are needed quickly for a capital project, and the government wants to avoid breaching an arbitrage agreement or paying high interest rates on bonds, it is likely to issue Bond Anticipation Notes. Until the capital project is completed, these notes may be rolled over so that new notes are issued to raise the money needed to pay off the old notes. In effect, the continual refinancing of Bond Anticipation Notes creates a long-term debt obligation. Therefore, once an issue of Bond Anticipation Notes is refinanced, it should be reported as a long-term debt.

Government bonds

Government bonds are debt obligations with long-term maturities. They are recorded at face value, and if they are sold at a premium or discount, that amount is recorded in a separate journal entry. The premium or discount is then amortized over the bond's life.

Popular types of government bonds include:
- *General Obligation Bonds:* These bonds are relatively safe investments, as repayment is government-guaranteed.
- *Revenue Bonds:* These bonds pose some risk to investors, as repayment comes from the revenues earned from the project funded by the bond issue. Therefore it does not have a government guarantee.
- *Refunding Bonds:* As interest rates drop, these bonds are issued to raise revenue to payoff debts with higher interest rates.

Amortizing bond premiums and discounts

Government bonds that are issued for a particular investor or a single investment group are typically offered at face value, but in the competitive market the bond price may rise above face value, known as a premium, or fall below face value, known as a discount. Bond premiums and discounts are to be amortized. The most favored method for determining the yearly amount to recognize is the Straight-line method. Using this method, the premium or discount amount is divided by the number of years till the bond matures to show the amortized yearly amount to be recognized. This amount is recorded as a reduction in expenses if it is part of a discount and as additional interest earned if it is part of a premium.

Amortizing bond issue costs

The costs associated with issuing bonds are regarded as prepaid expenses. They must be amortized. This is typically done using the Straight-line method which divides the costs by the bond life to determine the yearly amount to be recognized.

Sale of assets gains

To determine whether the sale of an asset has resulted in a gain or a loss, the difference between the asset's book value and the price it sold for must be found. If the sales price was greater than the book value, a gain is recorded as revenue. If the book value was greater than the sales price, a loss is recorded as an expense. Losses and gains from sold assets within fiduciary funds and proprietary funds are

- 23 -

reported on their operating statements, as well as, the government-wide operating statement.

Borrowed funds for assets

To acquire additional capital assets, the government may enter into a lease for the asset and make payments, or it may borrow the necessary funds from a third party to buy the capital asset. Either way, GAAP mandates that both transactions be reported in the same manner. The amount recorded is the lowest amount between the minimum lease payment and the capital asset's fair market value. This amount is recorded as a financing source and an expenditure in the governmental fund.

When a capital asset is sold, the proceeds are recorded by debiting Cash and crediting Other Financing Sources for the same amount.

Refunding bonds

When interest rates drop, this essentially means the cost of borrowing money has also dropped. Therefore, the government may now issue bonds at the lower interest rate, and use the money gained from the sale of these bonds to retire older bonds with higher interest rates. The newly issued bonds intended to raise money to retire older, more costly debt are known as refunding bonds. There are two methods for retiring the old debt:
- *Current Refunding:* The money raised from selling the new bond issue is used to immediately buy back the older bonds.
- *Advance Refunding:* The money raised from selling the new bond issue is invested and put into an escrow account to ensure funds are available for the retirement of an older bond issue.

U.S. Treasury securities types

These types of U.S. Treasury Securities:
- *Nonmarketable par value Treasury securities:* These are the U.S. Treasury's series of debt securities specifically meant to be issued to federal agencies at par value. These securities pose no threat of investment loss, as they are redeemed on demand at par value.
- *Market-based Treasury securities:* These are nonmarketable debt securities issued by the U.S. Treasury. Their prices and interest rates are matched with the going rate of the marketable Treasury debt securities.
- *Marketable Treasury Securities:* These are U.S. Treasury debt securities including bonds, notes and Treasury bills (T-bills) that are issued for the purpose of being publicly traded on security exchange markets.

All of these securities are recorded as assets at the price paid to acquire them. A premium is an amount paid over par value while a discount is the difference between par value and the sales price. Both premiums and discounts from security investments are required to be amortized using the interest method over the security's life. If a security is acquired by means other than money, it must be recorded at fair market value.

Capital contribution

The capital assets that one government contributes to another government are called capital contributions. A governmental fund would have no need to record a transaction involving a capital contribution because capital assets do not affect current financial resources. Proprietary and fiduciary funds would need to record a capital asset transaction. This would be done by debiting the capital asset account and crediting the capital contributions account. A proprietary fund would also report this type of activity on its Operating Statement while a fiduciary fund would report a capital contribution in its Change in Fund Net Assets Statement. Finally, the contribution would also need to be recognized at the government-wide level in the Statement of Activities.

Inventory

Recording inventories

- *Consumption method*: Used by funds that have a physical inventory, typically proprietary funds and enterprise, or business-type, funds. This method requires inventory items to be shown as assets up until the time they are shipped to customers, at which time they are expensed.
- *Purchases method*: Used by governmental funds. Since they usually do not have physical inventories, this method simply states that a good or service purchased by the fund should be expensed. This technique coincides with the current financial resources measurement focus used by governmental funds. If the fund does have an inventory, it may use the consumption method provided it complies with set conditions.

The First In, First Out (FIFO) method of valuing an inventory

Suppose multiple purchases of a particular product are made to maintain an inventory. If the First In, First Out (FIFO) method of valuing an inventory is used, then the inventory should be sold in the order it was received; the first shipment of goods received by the seller is the first goods sold to the customers. Products that are subject to spoilage or becoming obsolete are typically inventoried using the FIFO method. The in-stock inventory, as a result of this method, is valued on the balance sheet at the prices paid on the most recent inventory shipped.

If the cost of inventory increases over time, the in-stock inventory will be valued at the higher costs while the cost of goods sold will be valued at the lower costs. If the cost of inventory decreases over time, the in-stock inventory will be valued at the lower costs, and the cost of goods sold will be valued at the higher costs.

The Last In, First Out (LIFO) method of valuing inventory

Multiple purchases from manufacturers are necessary to maintain an inventory. Using the Last In, First Out (LIFO) method of valuing inventory, the most recent, or latest, shipment of inventory received is the first goods sold to customers. The value of the in-stock inventory shown on the balance sheet is based on the cost of the earliest items shipped. Therefore, current changes in the cost of inventory will not be reflected in the reported value of the in-stock inventory if it is determined using the LIFO method.

If the cost of inventory increases over time, the in-stock inventory will be reported at the lower costs, and the cost of goods sold will be shown at the higher costs. If the cost of inventory decreases, the in-stock inventory will be reported at the higher costs while the cost of goods sold will be valued at the lower costs.

Example: The difference between the FIFO and LIFO methods for valuing in-stock inventory and the cost of goods sold are shown in the following example: A state park purchases toy bears to be sold in their souvenir shop. In January, they buy 5 bears for $2 each. In February they buy 5 for $3 each. During the two months they sell 3 bears.

The differences between FIFO and LIFO are exemplified as follows:

Inventory Purchases

January	5 bears	$2 each
February	5 bears	$3 each

Total inventory (10 bears) – Goods sold (3 bears) = In-stock inventory (7 bears)

First In, First Out (FIFO) method:
Since the first bears received as inventory are the first bears sold, the cost of goods sold would be valued using the $2 price. The following values would be calculated:
Cost of goods sold = 3 bears x $2 = $6
In-stock inventory = (2 bears x $2) + (5 bears x $3) = $19

Last In, First Out (LIFO) method:
Since the last bears received as inventory are the first bears sold, the cost of goods sold would be valued using the $3 price. The following values would be calculated:
Cost of goods sold = 3 bears x $3 = $9
In-stock inventory = (2 bears x $3) + (5 bears x $2) = $16

The weighted average method for valuing inventory

As multiple purchases of an item are made to maintain an inventory of that item, a weighted average is calculated to determine the cost of the items. The weighted average is determined by adding the number of new inventory to the existing inventory and adding the total dollar amount of the new inventory to the total dollar amount of the existing inventory. The final total dollar amount is then divided by the final total number of inventory to arrive at the weighted average of the cost per unit, which is used to value the cost of goods sold. Unlike LIFO and FIFO, the timing of inventory purchases is irrelevant in calculating the cost of goods sold.

Example:

Initial inventory purchase...	5 toy bears x $2 each = $10
Second inventory purchase...	5 toy bears x $3 each = $15
Totals	10 toy bears $25

Weighted Average = Total cost of inventory / Total inventory =
$25 / 10 bears = $2.50 a bear

If 3 bears sold, the following values would be calculated:
Cost of goods sold = 3 bears x $2.50 = $7.50
In-stock inventory = 7 bears x $2.50 = $17.50

Property, plant and equipment

All physical assets with a useful life of at least two years that are obtained by a federal agency for the purpose of being used by that agency are recorded as "Property, Plant and Equipment". Examples of assets falling into this category include capital leased assets, leasehold improvements, land rights, and federal property used by another entity, such as a public university. This category of assets is recognized at the total cost of acquiring the asset, as well as, any additional costs incurred for making it ready for its intended use, such as labor and material costs or legal fees.

With the exception of stewardship property, all property, plant and equipment assets are depreciated over their useful lives. When the asset is no longer used by the agency, any remaining amount not yet depreciated is reported as a loss. The asset is then reclassified as an "asset held for sale", and it is recorded at its salvage value. When the asset sells, it is either recorded as a gain or a loss, depending on whether the final sales price was greater than or less than the asset's salvage value. If the sales price was greater than the salvage value, it would be reported as a gain. If the sales price was less than the salvage value, it would be reported as a loss.

Prepaid items

Prepaid items are items that are paid for before they are received or consumed, such as rent paid for the coming month. For governmental funds, prepaid items are usually recorded using the purchases method whereby they are recorded as expenditures. Although it is not commonly used, the consumption method is allowed. This method would record the prepaid items as an asset until it is used and then shown as an expense.

Claims and judgment

A *claim* is a request to receive compensation for damages incurred or to receive entitled benefits, as stated in a policy. A *judgment is* a court ordered or otherwise legally enforced claim.

Compensation that is paid to satisfy a claim or judgment is reported as a loss. The loss should be reported on the financial statements only when the following circumstances apply: the monetary value of the loss can be reasonably estimated, and it has created a liability or caused an asset to become impaired. If there is a possibility of a loss occurring due to a claim or judgment, it should be disclosed in the financial statements.

Judgments and claims are reported by all fund types. Proprietary and fiduciary funds report the amounts paid to satisfy a judgment or claim as an expense, and they recognize these expenses in the accounting period that the judgment or claim occurred. Governmental-wide statements report and recognize payments towards judgments and claims in the same manner. Governmental funds only report the amount of current financial resources used during the current accounting period to satisfy a judgment or claim. This amount is recorded as an expenditure. Since governmental funds' measurement focus differs from the governmental-wide statement's measurement focus, a reconciliation transaction is necessary for reporting governmental fund-levels' judgment claim payments on the government-wide Statement of Activities.

Contingent liabilities

Contingent liabilities are liabilities that may or may not occur depending upon the outcome of the circumstances, which involve events with a remote to probable chance of occurring. Often times it is not possible to determine a definite amount for a contingent liability. A common example of a contingent liability is a lawsuit. The reason a lawsuit creates a potential liability, and not a definite one, is because there are several possible outcomes:
- The case could be dismissed, and no liability would result.
- The case could go to trial, and the government could be found "not guilty". No liability would exist then.
- The case could go to trial, and the government could be found "guilty", in which case there would be a liability. However, unknown court costs, lawyer fees, and possibly punitive damages would make the liability amount indeterminable, until the case was closed.

Risk-financing activities

Risk-financing activities are transactions relating to risk management. Examples include buying property and liability coverage, making payments towards worker's compensation, and paying employee healthcare claims While either the general fund or the internal service fund may be chosen to handle such transactions, the internal service fund is favored since it requires less detailed information for completing transactions.

If the internal service fund is used, the proper claim recognition methods must be utilized to determine the total charges to other funds, using a time-adjusted actuarial method or a time-adjusted historical cost basis. This ensures revenues and expenses are balanced. Also the internal service fund should include a provision for losses of a catastrophic magnitude in its charges to other funds.

If the general fund is used, the government may choose any method for allocating charges to other funds. If the charges to other funds are greater than the general fund's actual risk-financing expenses, the excess amount is to be shown as transfers. Also, the general fund should pay claim expenses with current resources, thus recognizing these expenses immediately.

Insurance policies

To mitigate risk exposure, governments buy insurance. The purchase is recorded in whichever fund is handling the risk-financing activities; this would either be the general fund or the internal service fund. However, if the government is not the one primarily insured by the policy, the purchase is classified as a public entity risk pool and, therefore, recorded in an enterprise fund. The recording of insurance policies includes reporting premiums, losses, policy changes and contingencies. The premiums are accounted for as expenses. And finally, the necessity for disclosures is dependent upon risk levels.

Recognizing revenues

Derived tax revenues
Derived tax revenues are those revenues earned from government-imposed taxes. Under the accrual basis of accounting, the revenues, minus any refunds, are recorded when they are received. The modified accrual basis of accounting only recognizes revenues, minus any refunds, when they are readily available for spending.

Sources of derived tax revenues include:
- *Income tax revenues:* Come periodically from employers, as they withhold a portion of their employees' earned income and send it to the government. Also, individuals working on a per-fee basis or those self-employed submit income tax payments.
- *Sales tax revenue:* Comes from the sales tax charged on a merchant's goods and/or services. The merchant collects this tax from his customers and periodically sends the tax money to the government.

- *Sin tax:* Refers to the higher tax charged on specific products, such as cigarettes, gasoline, and alcohol. As with sales taxes, merchants collect the sin tax money when the product is sold and send the collected money to the government on a regular basis.

Property taxes and estate taxes

Property and estate taxes are sources of derived tax revenues. In order for the government to record an amount due as a receivable, it must have an enforceable claim.

As property taxes are paid, the revenue is recognized during the accounting period in which the government will be spending those revenues. Under the accrual method of accounting, the only property tax revenues recognized are those received during the current fiscal year. Under the modified accrual method, the recognition of property tax revenues is extended to include the 60 days following the year's end. Revenues received beyond those cut-off dates are accounted as deferred revenues. Estate tax revenues are recognized upon settlement of the estate.

Government-imposed fines

Members of the general public are subject to government-imposed fines if they break the law by either participating in an "act omitted", such as not paying taxes, or an "act committed", such as stealing.

The revenue from fines for minor offenses, such as a speeding ticket, is recognized when payment for the fine is received. If the offender chooses to bring the issue to court, revenue is not recognized until the case is closed. More serious offenses, in which someone is arrested, may result in revenues from bonds, as well as, fines, but the revenue is only recognizable when the person is found guilty.

The accrual accounting basis recognizes revenue to be generated from a fine the moment an enforceable claim is made and the fine is issued. However since this type of revenue is not subject to accrual and many fines go unpaid or have delinquent payments, many governments wait to recognize the revenue until it is actually received. The modified accrual accounting method recognizes the revenue once it is available for spending.

Key points on revenue recognition:
- Intergovernmental revenues from grants, entitlement payments, and shared revenues are recognized in a governmental fund during the fiscal period in which they are measurable and available. Also, any applicable eligibility requirements, as well as, any restrictions placed on the funds from their source must be met in order for them to be recognized. Failure to comply with stated requirements and restrictions may cause the funds to be forfeited in the case of entitlements and shared revenues.

- Proprietary funds recognize revenues from operating grants, discretionary grants, entitlements, and shared revenues as non-operating revenues until all of their restrictions and requirements have been met.
- Revenues generated from governmental or business-type activities are recorded as general revenue unless they can be directly linked to a function or program, in which case they are recorded as program revenues.

Intergovernmental revenue sources include:
- *Entitlement Payments:* Determined by an allocation formula, one government is entitled to payments from another government, known as entitlement payments. While these payments may or may not come with restrictions, they must comply with applicable laws and regulations.
- *Shared Revenues:* These are revenues that are paid to one government but must be shared with one or more other governments. An allocation formula is used to divide the funds fairly. Shared revenues must follow applicable laws and regulations.
- *Payments in lieu of Taxes:* A non-taxing government may receive payments from another government since it does not receive any tax revenue.

Donations

Private citizens and organizations may donate money or some other type of asset to a government or government agency. For fiduciary funds and proprietary funds, all donations are recognized and recorded in the period they are received. Governmental funds, which use a current financial resources measurement focus, only recognize donations when they cause a change in current assets. For example a cash donation would be recognized, whereas a donation of land would not be recognized because it does not affect current assets. If, however, the land was sold, the proceeds would increase current assets and would therefore be recognized. Donations that are designated for specific programs are classified and recorded as program revenue.

Collecting for another government

If a government or agency collects revenue on behalf of another government or agency, it must report the revenue as both an asset and a payable until it is transferred to the other government. It reports it as an asset because it physically has the funds and as a payable because it must give the funds to the other government.

Only governments and agencies that collect significant amounts of non-exchange revenue, which is deposited in the U.S. Treasury's general fund, and recipient governments or agencies are required to report a *Statement of Custodial Activity.* It must state the means by which the revenue was collected and spent. The reason custodial activities are reported separately is so the government's or agency's operating results are not compromised.

Social insurance programs

While government assistance programs have non-exchange transactions, and long-term pension programs have exchange transactions; federal social insurance programs have both non-exchange and exchange transactions. Therefore these types of programs, such as Social Security and Medicare, are accounted for separately and are required to submit a *Statement of Social Insurance.* This statement should include contributions and tax revenues earmarked for social programs, as well as, future benefits shown in present value. The necessity of converting future values into actuarial present values is to allow the public, many of whom are dependent upon social insurance programs, to be able to determine the program's future capabilities.

Entity versus non-entity assets

Entity assets are Interior-held assets that may be used to finance operations of the Interior. Non-entity assets are also assets that are held by the Interior; however, these assets may not be used towards the Interior's operational costs. These include assets that need to be appropriated or ones that are to be forwarded to the Department of Treasury at a later time. Federal agencies are to show both entity and non-entity assets on either the face of the balance sheet or in its notes.

Intragovernmental assets and liabilities refer to any assets or payments that are given to another government. Public liabilities refer to payments that are made to non-governmental entities. To comply with generally accepted accounting principles (GAAP), government agencies are to list their intragovernmental assets and liabilities separately from their public liabilities on the balance sheet.

Advances and prepayments

Advances are disbursements of cash towards a good or service that has not yet been provided. The government or agency shows cash advances as assets until the good or service has been provided. At that time, the advance is reduced while the service provided is expensed or the purchased good is shown as an asset.

Prepayments are monetary disbursements towards expenses which have yet to be incurred. The government or agency records prepayments as assets. Once the expense is incurred, the expense is recognized and the prepayment account is reduced.

Direct loans

Direct loans are loans offered directly by a federal agency. They typically charge lower interest rates than commercially offered loans for the purpose of encouraging citizens to partake in activities that promote the nation's general welfare. Examples include student loans and VA loans.

One major cost to the agency offering a direct loan is the difference in the agency's cost of borrowing funds and the rate of interest they receive from loaning those funds. For instance, the agency may borrow funds at a six percent annual rate, and then lend those funds at a four percent annual rate, thus creating an annual cost of two percent. Another major cost occurs when the borrower defaults on the loan. Since there are few credit requirements for the borrower to acquire a direct loan, these loans have a high risk level of default.

Government loan guarantees

A loan guarantee is the government's guarantees regarding particular loan terms to a public entity, such as a bank or financial firm. A common example is the government's guarantee to a bank that it will pay the difference between the bank's borrowing interest rate and its lower lending rate. So if the bank borrows at an eight percent interest rate and loans those same funds at a six percent interest rate, the government might offer a two percent loan guarantee. As the government makes these payments, they are recorded as liabilities at the loan's present value. Loan guarantees are periodically reviewed so the liabilities may be reduced for loans in default, as well as, loans that have matured.

Events recognized and recorded

Government related events refer to liabilities that result from the federal government's interaction with its surrounding environment. This includes legal claims against negligent acts of the government or agents of the government. The liability is recorded at the time of the event; if the amount cannot be measured, it is recorded once it is measurable.

Government acknowledged events refer to liabilities that are financial consequences resulting from the government's acknowledgement of certain events. Such liabilities are recorded in the amount the government holds itself financially responsible. These types of liabilities are only recognized after the following has occurred:
- The event was acknowledged by the president.
- Resources have been appropriated and authorized towards the event by Congress.
- An exchange took place or non-exchange amounts are payable.

Post-employment plans

Employee pension plan offered by governments

For accounting purposes, pensions are classified as fiduciary activities. From the many different types of pension plans, governments typically choose to offer a defined benefit plan, allowing them to inform their employees, with certainty, the benefits they may expect upon retirement. Employee contributions to a pension are recorded as assets. When an employee retires or meets the eligibility requirements for retirement, the pension must be recognized as a liability, and payments to the employee commences.

Occasionally, cost-sharing pension plans or multiple employer plans are offered. Governmental funds consider contributions to these types of pension plans to be expenditures. Proprietary funds record the contributions as expenses.

Trusts

Post-employment benefit plans that are administered as trusts must submit additional information regarding their current financial activities and net assets in comparison to other post-employment benefit plans. More specifically, the additional information should include two-year financial statements, containing a Statement of Plan Net Assets and a Statement of Changes in Plan Net Assets, and also two schedules showing data from multiple years. The plan's assets and liabilities and the assets held by the trust are reported in the Statement of Plan Net Assets. Any change in net assets, such as a decrease due to benefits paid, would be reported in the Statement of Changes in Plan Net Assets. The financial statement notes should have a brief explanation of the benefit plan and the accounting policies used, as well as, the amount of contributions made to the plan and the amount to be held in reserves to meet legal requirements. The current status of the plan's funding and the valuation methods used should also be disclosed.

Actuarial valuation

The frequency of which post-employment benefit plans receive actuarial valuations depends on its membership size:

- Valuation occurs every two years when there are two hundred or more participants.
- Valuation occurs every three years when there are less than two hundred participants.
- If there are less than one hundred participants, an alternative measurement method may be used. This would be a simplified actuarial valuation process, not requiring a specialist.

A measurement report is required to accompany the actuarial valuations. The purpose of it is to reveal when the valuation took place, to explain the methods used, and to disclose allowable assumptions, such as healthcare costs and caps on benefits.

<u>Not administered as a trust and defined contribution</u>

A post-employment benefit plan offering a defined benefit plan that is not administered as a trust or trust equivalent but does include other employers is to be reported as an agency fund. All employers in this type of plan share the administrative costs. An overview of the plan, its main accounting principles, and data regarding contributions are expected to be disclosed in the notes of the plan.

If a defined contribution plan is the basis of the post-employment benefit plan, then the same financial reporting requirements apply as for fiduciary funds and fiduciary component units.

Retirement and unused days

If a government employee retires from his job before using all of his vacation days, he is paid for those days. The transaction is recorded as an expense for the current accounting period.

Whether the employee is paid for unused sick days depends on the government's policy. A policy that allows employees to be compensated for accrued sick days would require the accounting records to show a liability until those days are either used or the employee retires, at which time the payment to the employee would be expensed. To determine their liability, the government uses historical data to estimate how many employees will be retiring. A policy that only gives sick pay on the days an employee calls in sick would eliminate the need for recording a liability. In this case, a retired employee would not receive sick day compensation.

Reporting

Financial statements

Two types of financial statements:
- *Balance Sheet:* The balance sheet is the financial statement showing the government or government agency's assets, liabilities, and net position for a particular time period.
- *Statement of Net Costs:* The Statement of Net Costs reports the government or government agency's net costs of operations. The gross cost of each major component and program is required to be shown. Previously, the costs of goods and services that were provided to other government bodies and programs were reported separately, but today they are expected to be disclosed in the footnotes belonging to the Statement of Net Costs.

The government issues two main types of financial statements: the government-wide financial statements and fund financial statements. The government-wide financial statements report on the overall financial condition of the government in its entirety, with the exception of fiduciary activities which are excluded. They show net assets, using an accrual basis of accounting. The fund financial statements report fund balances. Funds are individual reporting entities containing their own set of assets and liabilities. Major funds are reported individually while smaller funds are combined and reported as a single entity. The accounting basis used depends on the type of fund; proprietary funds are accounted for on an accrual basis, governmental funds use a modified accrual basis, and fiduciary funds may use either an accrual or modified accrual basis. Notes accompany both types of financial statements to provide additional information and important disclosures.

Comprehensive annual financial report components
Components of the comprehensive annual financial report include:
- *Introduction:* This area provides basic information. For example, it typically includes a title page, the table of contents, a letter of transmittal, the organizational structure of the government entity, and a list of government officials. The letter of transmittal explains accounting standards that have been used, projected goals, the reporting responsibilities of management, and local economic conditions. It also includes a description of assumed and mitigated risks, an explanation of the internal controls over the management of cash, an independent audit, and finally any awards.
- *Financials:* The financial statements with accompanying information, the auditor's report, and any other relevant financial information are the contents of this section.

- *Statistics:* This section provides statistical data on the government's current economical state in compliance with the GASB Codification Section 2800 statistical tables.
- *Financial Trends:* Changes in net assets are reported in this section to allow report users to evaluate how efficiently funds were handled.

External financial reports

A government or government agency conveys its fiscal year's operation results and its overall financial position to the general public and investors through its external financial reports. More specifically, the operating results are revealed in the operating statement which shows revenues and expenses, along with the difference between the two, commonly known as the "bottom line". The government or government agency's financial position may be assessed from its statement of net assets, which is similar to a balance sheet. It shows the government's assets, liabilities, and equity, including fund balances.

Information found in an external financial report includes:
- *Revenue Capacity*: This includes the most recent ten years' information about the government's revenues, such as the main source of revenues, the revenue base, and its rates.
- *Debt Capacity*: This pertains to debt from all areas – governmental activities, business-type activities, and general overall government debt. It includes debt amounts, debt ratios, overlapping debt, limitations, and the amount of revenues set aside to cover outstanding debts.
- *Demographics and Economics*: This includes the following data for the most recent ten years: unemployment rates, per capita income (totals and averages), and the locations of major employers.
- *Operations:* Such information as the number of government employees, descriptions of capital assets and their usage, and operating indicators is found in this area of the external financial report, along with the methods used for obtaining the reported information.
- *Explanatory Narrative*: This supplements the statistical section, explaining basic concepts, goals, factors causing out-of-the-ordinary results, and the correlation of certain statistics to other areas of the report.

Government-wide financial statements

The government-wide financial statements use the economic resources measurement focus and accrual basis of accounting. Enterprise funds and activities relating to enterprise funds are reported as business-type activities with their transactions also being recorded and reported using the economic resources measurement focus and the accrual basis of accounting. Governmental funds and activities, however, use the current financial resources measurement focus and the modified accrual basis of accounting. Since these methods differ from those used on the government-wide financial statements, it is necessary to use adjusting accounting entries to convert the focus for the financial statements.

Summary financial reporting

Summary financial reporting has also been called popular reporting, as it is intended for the general public since more and more citizens and individual investors have an increased interest in the government's financial state. It is designed to be user-friendly with an easy-to-follow structure. Accompanying charts and graphs allow for a simple interpretation of the financial data or may be used as a quick reference.

Along with all of the government reports, the summary financial information includes a condensed version of the financial statements and summary reports. These additional reports merely supplement the Comprehensive Annual Financial Report. They are in no way meant to replace it, as they are not regulated by the GASB.

Report major component units

Major component units of a government, such as a landfill or a public school system, may be reported in one of the following ways:
- Each major component unit is shown on the government-wide Statement of Net Assets and Statement of Activities in its own separate column.
- Statements of the major component units are combined on the basic financial statements after the fund financial statements. This aggregate total is then reported on the government-wide financial statement as "component units".
- The major component units may be listed in the condensed financial statements and found in the notes accompanying the complete financial statements.
- Also, if any significant transactions took place in the component unit during the fiscal year, they should be reported.

Interperiod equity user fees

Interperiod equity is the Governmental Accounting Standards Board's (GASB's) recommended objective that a government only offers services to the extent that it has revenues to pay for the costs of those services within a specified time frame, typically a year. If it offers more services than it can afford, taxpayers will be burdened with this debt in the future. To continue offering services when revenues from federal, state, or local taxes cannot cover the expenses, a government agency may charge a user fee to citizens using the service. Examples of government fees include admission to a city pool or state park, and those required for obtaining building permits. 17a. Explain how a government user fee is calculated.

The following formula may be used in determining a government user fee:
   User Fee = (Total Fixed Costs / # of Expected Users) + Variable Costs per person

Fixed costs are those that will remain the same whether there is one user or one hundred users; examples include the building and office equipment. Variable costs are those that are dependent upon the number of users, such as the DMV's cost of producing driver's licenses varies in relation to the number of citizens needing new driver's licenses.

Example: Suppose a city installs a community pool and must determine a user fee. It calculates all its fixed costs (i.e., the cost of the pool, landscaping, employee wages, etc.) to be $90,000 and its variable cost of pool and grounds maintenance to be $2 a person. They expect to have 15,000 users.

The user fee would be calculated as:

User Fee = ($90,000 / 15,000 people) + $2 per person

User Fee = $6 per person + $2 per person = $8 per person

External factors

Since governments are obligated to promote the social and economic welfare of society, it is important for them to take other factors into account and adjust the calculated user fee accordingly. Such factors include:

- *Socio-economic environment*: If a user fee is so high that citizens with low incomes cannot afford the government service the fee may be lowered so that it is available to all citizens.
- *Competitive environment*: The fee should be set fairly against private businesses that offer similar services, as cities want to encourage business growth, not force them out-of-business. On the other hand, government agencies have to stay competitive with other government agencies offering similar services in nearby cities; otherwise they may lose patrons and revenue to them.

Modified approach for infrastructure

The modified approach for infrastructure allows eligible infrastructure assets to not be depreciated, as those assets have proven to be in better-than-average condition. To qualify for use of the modified approach, three requrements must be fulfilled: 1) the infrastructure's inventory must be current, 2) the asset's condition must be assessed using a measurable scale, and 3) the measurable level which considers the condition to be better-than-average must be disclosed. Also, to maintain eligibility, the asset must be assessed, at a minimum, every three years.

Supplementary reporting is required when the modified approach for infrastructure is used. Some of the information that should be included in the required reporting includes: the three most recent condition assessments and the dates of those assessments, as well as, the estimated annual cost for the government to maintain the asset in better-than-average condition, and the last five years' comparisons of the estimated and actual maintenance costs.

SEA reports

A Service Efforts and Accomplishments report measures exactly that – the efforts and accomplishments of a government agency's services or programs.
- The measure of efforts, or inputs, calculates the amount of money budgeted and actual funds put toward a goal, such as expenses for materials, employees, and advertising. Non-financial information may be included in the measurement of efforts, as well.
- The measure of accomplishments measures outputs, both expected and actual number of goods and services offered, and studies the outcome of the services, determining what they have accomplished and what benefits have resulted.
- The cost-outcome measurement determines the cost of an agency's accomplishments on a per unit basis.

All of these measurements allow SEA report users to determine whether the agency's program goals are being met and to evaluate which programs are operating efficiently. However, the main purpose of SEA reports is to use the information as a whole to evaluate the government agency's overall performance. It also serves as a record of the agency's accountability.

A SEA report should have the following qualities:
- *Relevant:* The report should contain current information related to the objectives of a government agency and its programs.
- *Understandable*: The information should be presented in a clear, easy-to-follow format and provide a description of the factors effecting an agency's performance.
- *Reliable*: All data should be true, consistent, and verifiable.
- *Timely*: The information should be reported and distributed within a reasonable time period.
- *Consistent:* The data should be gathered and reported using the same method for each reporting period.
- *Comparable*: The information should be displayed in a similar format so reports from different periods or agencies may be easily compared.

Limitations
While the SEA report may indicate which programs are successful and which are failures, it does not explain the reasons for their success or failure. Also it does not describe the program's methods or strategies for reaching its goals; nor does it give enough information to determine if those goals are even attainable or appropriate.

To help users work around these limitations, the report should contain a statement suggesting that the report be used with supplementary information. This would help further explain the report's data. Also anything affecting an agency's performance that is outside of its control should be mentioned in the report. Finally, the report may be more useable and may allow for a more analytical review if the data is segregated by geographic location, department, facility, or some other logical division.

Management Discussion and Analysis report

The purpose of the Management Discussion and Analysis report is to provide a user-friendly summary of a government's financial statements. It is also a means for governments to explain how their basic financial statements relate to the government-wide financial statements. Under the Government Accounting Standards Board (GASB) Statement Number 34, this report is required supplementary information. The content of the report has the following general requirements for inclusion:

- A condensed version of the financial statements accompanied by a brief summary of them
- A description of the year's ending financial position and a comparison of it to the previous year's financial results. The year-to-year changes, both negative and positive, should be explained.
- An explanation for the differences in the General Fund's estimated and actual budgeted amounts
- A list of long-term debt and significant capital assets
- Individual fund balances and transactions

Statement of Net Assets

The government-wide Statement of Net Assets first reports assets, which are placed in the order of their liquidity. The most liquid assets are shown first. A classified statement is commonly used to segregate the long-term and short-term assets. Next, the liabilities are listed. Short-term liabilities, those with a maturity date of less than a year, are reported separately from long-term liabilities, which are those with a maturity date greater than a year. The long-term liabilities are further categorized by those maturing and being due in the current year, and those which are not maturing until after the year.

Total liabilities are subtracted from total assets to arrive at net assets. The net assets must be grouped as follows: "invested in capital assets, net of related debt", "restricted assets", and "unrestricted assets". The aggregate of these groupings equals total net assets.

Components of net assets on the government-wide Statement of Net Assets include:
- *Invested in Capital Assets, Net of Related Debt*: This shows the value of capital assets without any accumulated depreciation and without the outstanding debts related to the acquisition, construction, or improvement of the capital assets. When the amount of unspent revenues meant for a capital asset is significant, they should not be used to report a reduction in outstanding debt, but rather they should be reported as unrestricted assets.

- 41 -

- *Restricted Assets:* Assets that have legal or regulatory restrictions on their use, including assets that creditors, grantors, or contributors have lent or given to the government to be used for a specific purpose. This should not be confused with the "fund balance reservation" which are assets set aside by the government's choice for a specific purpose. On the Statement of Net Costs, restricted assets should be categorized as "expendable" and "non-expendable".
- *Unrestricted Assets:* All other assets that are free from restrictions and obligations.

Statement of Activities

General guidelines for the Statement of Activities include:
- To report the fiscal year's operating costs and revenues, as well as, to clearly depict the dependency of individual activities on tax revenues, the Statement of Activities uses the net cost format.
- A simple description of the governmental activities and their purposes should be included.
- Both the economic cost and net cost of services is to be on the statement.

Rules on reporting direct, indirect, and depreciation expenses on the Statement of Activities include:
- Direct expenses should be reported according to the function to which they are directly linked.
- If a depreciation expense can be linked to a particular function, it should be included as a direct expense.
- If a depreciation expense cannot be directly linked to a function or if a depreciation expense results from a shared capital asset, it may either be reported as part of the general government fund or it may be given its own separate line.
- Indirect expenses are listed in a separate column.

On the Statement of Activities, revenues are categorized into one of these three main sections:
- *Charges for services:* These are revenues received in exchange for services, such as payments received from permit fees.
- *Operating grants and/or contributions:* These are revenues designated to specified programs.
- *Capital grants and/or contributions:* These revenues should be recorded as restricted assets and should only be used for the specified programs for which they are designated.

It should be noted that if earnings from any investments of restricted funds or endowments have contractual or agreed upon restrictions, they should be reported

FREE Study Skills DVD Offer

Dear Customer,

Thank you for your purchase from Mometrix! We consider it an honor and privilege that you have purchased our product and want to ensure your satisfaction.

As a way of showing our appreciation and to help us better serve you, we have developed a Study Skills DVD that we would like to give you for <u>FREE</u>. **This DVD covers our "best practices" for studying for your exam, from using our study materials to preparing for the day of the test.**

All that we ask is that you email us your feedback that would describe your experience so far with our product. Good, bad or indifferent, we want to know what you think!

To get your **FREE Study Skills DVD**, email <u>freedvd@mometrix.com</u> with "FREE STUDY SKILLS DVD" in the subject line and the following information in the body of the email:

   a. The name of the product you purchased.

   b. Your product rating on a scale of 1-5, with 5 being the highest rating.

   c. Your feedback. It can be long, short, or anything in-between, just your impressions and experience so far with our product. Good feedback might include how our study material met your needs and will highlight features of the product that you found helpful.

   d. Your full name and shipping address where you would like us to send your free DVD.

If you have any questions or concerns, please don't hesitate to contact me directly.

Thanks again!

Sincerely,

Jay Willis
Vice President
<u>jay.willis@mometrix.com</u>
1-800-673-8175

The World's #1 Test Preparation Company

as program revenues. If they do not have restrictions, they should be reported as general revenues.

Definitions of items found on the Statement of Activities:
- *Special Item:* An event or transaction that is unusual or occurs infrequently. It must be significant, but still under management's control.
- *Extraordinary Item:* An event or transaction that is both, unusual and occurs infrequently.

On the Statement of Activities, "Special Items" are reported separately after "General Revenues". "Extraordinary Items" are also reported separately, and they follow "Special Items". Events or transactions that are unusual or infrequent but do not qualify as a special item because they are out of the management's control should be reported separately near "Special Items".

The Governmental Accounting Standards Board (GASB) Statement Number 34 states that interfund receivables and payables for governmental funds and enterprise funds no longer need to be reported on the Statement of Activities. Only the difference between interfund payables and interfund receivables of the governmental and enterprise activities should be included in the internal balances on the Statement of Activities. It should be noted that internal balances are no longer shown in the primary government's total column.

Interfund transactions pertaining to fiduciary funds are still expected to be reported. They are recorded as "payable to (external party)" or "receivable from (external party)".

While transfers between governmental and enterprise activities are no longer required to be reported on the Statement of Activities, outstanding transfers between the two are expected to be reported and are done so in the same manner as interfund receivables and payables.

Where internal service funds are reported on the Statement of Activities depends on the internal service funds' primary customers. If an internal service fund's primary customers are mostly connected to governmental activities, then they are reported under governmental activities on the Statement of Activities. If the internal service fund's primary customers are mostly connected to business-type activities, then they are reported with enterprise activities on the Statement of Activities. The net revenue of an internal service fund should be near zero a significant balance would show that the service fee being charged is too high, and a large deficit would indicate that the fee being charged is too low. Also on the Statement of Activities, investment income and interest expense are reported with governmental activities, and additional earned revenues are classified as program revenues.

Consolidated Balance Sheet

The standard organization of a Consolidated Balance Sheet begins with "Assets". The first sub-heading is "Intragovernmental Assets" under which is a list of the Treasury's fund balances, net investments, and other intragovernmental assets. The sum of this list is shown as "Total Intragovernmental Assets". Next is a listing of assets, including cash, investments, interest receivables, and loan receivables. Finally, "Total Assets" is calculated and reported.

The second major category is "Liabilities". Intergovernmental liabilities, such as deferred revenue and custodial liabilities, among others, are listed under "Intergovernmental Liabilities". A total for the list is shown, and common liabilities, such as accounts payable and employee benefits due, follow. The "Total Liabilities" are revealed. Then there is a place for "Commitments and Contingencies", followed by "Net Position", which shows "Unexpended Appropriations" and "Cumulative Results of Operations". The tabulation for "Total Net Position" is reported. Finally, "Total Liabilities and Net Position" is shown.

Statement of Net Costs

A federal agency's Statement of Net Costs should report information that is consistent with the goals and objectives stated in the Management's Discussion and Analysis report. For example, the gross costs and anticipated earned revenues for the goals stated in the Management's Discussion and Analysis should be shown in the Statement of Net Costs. Also the full costs of all relevant government programs should be included in the Statement of Net Costs, along with, which of the programs' net costs are to be financed by budgetary resources or by other sources. The information should be provided in a user-friendly format.

Revenues that are required to be reported

The SFFAC No. 2 specifies that a government agency must show the revenues earned from each of its programs and organizations on its Statement of Net Costs. Those revenues should include:

- All the programs' and organizations' revenues earned in exchange for the goods/services they provided.
- Revenues received from "inherently governmental service" which are then applied towards the service's administrative costs. Such revenues should be deducted from the organization's total cost.
- Incidental revenues
- Insignificant revenues should be disclosed in the notes to the statement.
- Revenues earned from non-specific programs
- Revenues obtained from other government agency activities need to be reported on a separate form from the reporting of revenues obtained from non-federal agencies.

<u>Costs that are required to be reported</u>
The Statement of Federal Financial Accounting Concepts No. 2 mandates that costs on the Statement of Net Costs be properly grouped into cost categories. It also specifies the costs that should be included in the statement as:

- Costs directly associated with a particular program or organization.
- Costs necessary for maintaining the operations of the program or organization, even if those costs are not directly related to a specific program or organization.
- Program administration and management costs.
- Costs incurred from other government agency activities must be reported on a separate form from the reporting of costs incurred from non-federal agencies.

Comparative statement

A comparative statement is required in the Statement of Net Costs to match the government or government agency's stated goals and objectives with their accomplishments and efforts toward meeting those goals and objectives. Any changes in the goals or strategies for achieving those goals should be acknowledged. The goals of each of the government or government agency's sub-organizations, also known as component units, should also be given. The Statement of Net Costs should allow users to determine the relative costs of each component unit. Detailed information about the sub-organizations, or component units, is found elsewhere in their own financial reports.

Note disclosures

Disclosures in the notes to the financial statements are not only important to the user, but they are also often required. They provide necessary financial details which make the government or government agencies' finances more understandable. They may also discuss broader issues which have an overall impact on the finances of the government or agency. Whether the note disclosures give specific financial details or address broader issues, their main purpose is to give a clearer understanding of the government or government agency's operations. Typical note disclosures include: fund balance of Treasury, net taxes receivable, net investments, direct loans, loan guarantees, cash, and asset and liability analyses.

Operating Performance Report

The Operating Performance Report shows the management of assets and liabilities, allowing users to assess how effective the federal agency was at attaining its stated goals. More specifically the report should include information regarding the use of: cash, loans, loan guarantees, receivables, inventory maintenance, supply inventories, estimated liabilities, estimated market value of forfeited assets, management of forfeited assets, unpaid expenses, and any changes in a program's cost. It should also provide the following *objective* information: program costs, cost comparisons between programs, workloads, unit costs, total marginal costs/benefits, financial/non-financial indicators of inputs and outputs, and a breakdown of a program's total costs, revealing direct and indirect costs, as well as, full and incremental costs. The report's information allows users to determine how the agency acquired its resources, what resources were used in specific programs, and how those resources were managed to meet the agency's goals.

Statement of Custodial Activities

If a government agency is formed for the purpose of collecting revenues that are meant for financing the government's general operations, that agency is obligated to file a Statement of Custodial Activities according to the Statement of Federal Financial Accounting Concepts No. 2. The following items should be reported in the Statement of Custodial Activities:
- Revenue-generating sources
- Changes in "amounts due" to the agency which have yet to be collected.
- Transferred amounts that are still retained by the agency.
- Changes in transferred amounts

Incidental revenue that has been collected should be reported in the statement's footnotes. While amounts temporarily held by the agency or on behalf of another agency are reported in Assets and Liabilities, they are not to be reported in the Statement of Custodial Activities.

Statement of Budgetary Resources

Budgetary resources refer to funds or other resources that are immediately available for the government agency to use currently or in the future. According to the Statement of Federal Financial Accounting Concepts No. 2, the Statement of Budgetary Resources should include: the Budget Authority, remaining unobligated resources from prior periods, reimbursements, adjustments, and the status of budgetary resources. The contents of the status of budgetary resources reports how budgetary resources were spent, remaining unobligated resources from prior periods, obligations incurred, and the outlay of resources to reduce or pay off those obligations. The financial data and information supplied in the Statement of Budgetary Resources should be complied and reported in compliance with GAAP.

Statement of Program Performance Measures

The Office of Management and Budgets (OMB) requires auditors of government agency financial statements to assess controls over the program performance measures of agencies. Auditors often use the Statement of Program Performance Measures as a source to help fulfill this duty. The Statement of Program Performance Measures reports output and/or outcome performance measures, as well as, other selected performance measures over the agency's major programs. A comparison of the current period's measures with those from prior periods makes the report more useful by showing areas of improving or declining performance and is therefore required. It is suggested that agencies take into consideration the recommendations of external report users, such as budget examiners and congressmen and their staff, when making the selection of which performance measures to report. Also, the chosen performance measures should correlate to the purpose and goals of the programs.

The objectives of program performance measures and the reporting thereof are as follows:
- *Complete:* Do the performance measures fully address all of the agency's goals and objectives?
- *Legitimate:* Are the performance measures useful to external report users?
- *Understandable:* Is the format and content of the report understandable to external, as well as, internal users?
- *Comparable:* Does the reporting format allow for similar programs to be easily compared?
- *Consistent:* Are the performance measures reported in a consistent manner each reporting period? Are incurred cost measurements consistent with inputs and outputs/outcomes?
- *Timely:* Are the Performance Measurement Reports issued in time to still be relevant?
- *Reliable:* Is the reported data accurate, reliable, and verifiable?

The answer to each checklist question should be "yes". If it is not, the agency should make improvements to their reporting process.

Changes in Net Position

The Statement of Changes in Net Position reports the total results of operations. This includes the operation's financing sources, such as appropriations, royalties, non-exchange revenues and judgment payments from the Department of Treasury. Along with appropriations, unused appropriations and the net amount of appropriations should be reported. Financing costs that are attributed to the reporting federal agency must be recognized on this statement despite the fact that another federal agency is paying them. Changes in operations must be acknowledged in the report. Disclosure of prior period adjustments is required in the financial statement's notes.

Consolidated Statement of Changes in Net Position

The Consolidated Statement of Changes in Net Position has two major sections: unexpended appropriations and cumulative results of operations. Unexpended appropriations are appropriations that have either not been obligated or have yet to be spent due to undelivered orders. The first line under the heading "Unexpended Appropriations" is the *beginning balance*, followed by the *budgetary financing sources*. These sources should show the amount of appropriations that were received, used, and transferred to somewhere else. The *net change* is then displayed, and finally the *ending balance for unexpended appropriations* is tabulated.

The Consolidated Statement of Changes in Net Position has two major sections: unexpended appropriations and cumulative results of operations. The second major section shows a beginning balance under the heading of "Cumulative results of Operations". The overall effect of *prior period adjustments* is then given, followed by *changes in accounting methods*. The result is shown as the *adjusted beginning balance*. Next, *budgetary financial resources*, such as royalties retained and non-exchange revenue is listed. *Other financing sources*, such as costs that are covered by others, are then given. The financing sources are totaled and the *net cost of operations* is reveled, followed by the *net change*, and finally the *ending balance for cumulative results of operations*. It should be noted that a disclosure about the prior period adjustment should be included in the notes of the Consolidated Statement of Changes in Net Position.

The Statement of Federal Financial Accounting Concepts No. 2 identifies the following items that should be reported on the Statement of Net Changes in Position:

- Net costs covered by other revenues
- Appropriations spent on specific organizations or programs
- Non-exchange revenues
- Private donations to the agency from citizens
- Unreimbursed transfers *to* the agency from another government agency
- Unreimbursed transfers *from* the agency to other government agencies
- Any agency costs that are paid by another government agency
- Prior period adjustments
- Any changes in the amount of unspent appropriations
- The period's beginning net position
- The period's ending net position

Statement of Financing

The purpose for the Statement of Financing is to present, in user-friendly terms, net costs according to GAAP and budgetary obligations. The information contained in the report is not provided in any of the other financial statements. It displays budgetary resources obligated and lists other resources; together, they show total resources used to finance activities. Then resources used to finance items not part of the net cost of operations are listed. The difference between the two totals reveals the total resources used to finance the net cost of operations. Reconciliation between proprietary and budgetary activities and balances must also be in the Statement of Financing.

Custodial credit risk

Custodial credit risk exists for cash deposits when there is a possibility that the financial institution will fail or if it actually does, causing the government to lose its cash deposit or other collateral securities. Cash deposits are subjected to custodial credit risk when:

- The funds have not been insured by the FDIC (Federal Depository Insurance Corporation).
- There has been no collateral given for the funds or securities deposited.
- The collateral for the funds or securities is held by the same financial institution.
- The collateral for the funds or securities is held by the trust department of the issuing financial institution but not in the government's name.

By the end of the fiscal year, if any deposits of cash or securities are exposed to custodial credit risk, they should be fully disclosed.

Disclosure notes for investments

It is necessary to provide disclosure notes for investments. They should reveal any restrictions, legal requirements, and risks imposed on the investments. Organized by investment type, investments in the following areas require full disclosure: governmental activities, enterprise activities, individual major funds, minor funds (reported cumulatively), and fiduciary funds with a greater-than-average exposure to risk. The types of risk that should be disclosed include: custodial risk, interest rate risk, foreign currency risk, and credit risk. For credit risk, it is only mandatory for investments that are five percent or greater than the total amount of investments to disclose their credit risk exposure.

Securities lending transactions

The Governmental Accounting Standards Board (GASB) Codification Section 160 explains how to account and report transactions involving the lending of securities. According to it, the securities involved in transactions in which they are lent or transferred to broker-dealers and collateral is received are reported on the government's balance sheet as assets. If the collateral received is securities that the government may sell whether the borrower is in default or not, the collateral is also reported as an asset. If the collateral received is securities that the government may only sell or pledge when the borrower is in default, the collateral should not be reported on the balance sheet as an asset or liability. Any liabilities that do result from a securities lending transaction should be reported on the balance sheet.

Recording investment values

Governments and their agencies record the investment value of nonparticipating contracts and some money market accounts as an amortized cost on the balance sheet. However, investments in external investment pools and other specified investments are required to be reported at fair value on the balance sheets according to the Governmental Accounting Standards Board (GASB) Statement Number 31. Changes in the fair value of investments, as well as, investment income are reported on the Operating Statement as revenues. It is necessary to include information on an investment's fair value at year-end and the carrying amount in the disclosure notes.

Accounts receivable

Definitions relating to accounts receivable:
- *Receivable Recognition and Measurement Focus Basis of Accounting*: This addresses the proper timing of when to recognize and record accounts receivable. Both the accrual basis and the modified accrual basis of accounting follow the same guidelines for recognizing receivables.
- *Exchange Transactions*: A transaction in which fees are charged in exchange for a service to be rendered. Receivables are recognized at the time of the exchange.
- *Exchange-like Transactions*: Examples of exchange-like transactions include a citizen paying a fee for a permit or license. Again, receivables are recognized at the time of the exchange.
- *Non-exchange Transactions*: A transaction in which no exchange takes place; goods and/or services are rendered without charging a fee. This type of transaction must be classified according to the government's ability to afford the service or good it is providing, which may be through grants, donations, and shared revenues.
- *Derived Tax Revenue Transaction*: Transactions in which citizens pay a government-imposed tax, such as state sales taxes or federal income taxes. A derived tax revenue transaction is recorded either at the time of the exchange or when the revenues are received, whichever happens first.
- *Imposed Non-exchange Revenue Transactions*: Transactions in which there is no exchange offered for the government-imposed assessment. The transaction is recognized when the government obtains a legal claim or when it receives money or resources, whichever happens first.

Exchange and exchange-like transactions

Exchange transactions are purchasing transactions in which money is exchanged for a good or service, such as an amount paid for water/sewer service; whereas exchange-like transactions are transactions in which money is given to receive the privilege or authorization to do something. An example of an exchange-like transaction would be a fee being paid for a driver's license or building permit.

The accounting method used dictates how revenue received from these types of transactions is recorded:

- *Accrual basis of accounting:* Revenue is recognized as the exchange occurs.
- *Modified accrual basis of accounting:* Revenue is recognized once it is available for use.
- *Cash basis of accounting:* Revenue is recognized as it is received.

Non-exchange transactions

A government mandated non-exchange transaction occurs when one government furnishes resources or the use of resources to another government. A voluntary non-exchange transaction takes place between two or more willing participants who enter into a legislative agreement or a contract. In both cases, the providing government may place restrictions on the use and purpose of its resources, and the following conditions must be met in these types of transactions:

- The receiving government possesses the qualities that the providing government designates as necessary.
- Time requirements established by the provider are respected by the recipient.
- An expenditure driven grant is established, meaning the provider determines which resources may be given or used by the recipient on a reimbursement basis.
- Any contingencies established by the provider must be appeased by the recipient.

Once these conditions are met, the receivable may be recognized.

Government transactions that do not involve a direct exchange, such as money given for a good/service, are considered non-exchange transactions. These types of transactions involve the government receiving revenues from: taxes, donations, fines, and grants. The recognition and recording of revenues from non-exchange transactions is as follows:

- Tax revenues received in no-exchange circumstances (i.e., property tax revenues) are recognized once the government has a legal claim.
- Revenues from grants are recognized once all of the grant requirements are met.
- Revenues from donations are recognized once specific conditions have been met.
- Tax revenues from quasi-exchange transactions such as state sales tax revenues, are recorded as follows, when using:
  - *Accrual basis:* Revenues are recognized at the time of the quasi-exchange.

- o *Modified accrual basis:* Revenues are recognized as the funds become available.
- o Cash basis: Revenues are recognized as they are received.

Accounts receivable allowances

Receivables are reported absent of allowances and discounts. If a receivable has been recorded on the financial statements, but later it is determined that the collection of the receivable is doubtful; the estimated amount that is considered uncollectible should be recorded as an allowance for doubtful accounts. If there is uncertainty surrounding the amount that may be uncollectible, one of two methods may be used to determine an amount: the percentage of receivables method or the percentage of sales method.

In the case of loans, historical data should be reviewed to determine which types of loans have a higher-than-average default rate so that allowance accounts may be adjusted to accommodate the higher probability of default. Loans that do not require repayment but rather require the recipient to follow specified loan provisions do not need to establish a receivable account. If the recipient fails to follow the loan provisions, then a receivable account should be established.

Accounts receivable and government refunds

If the government receives an overpayment, it must issue a refund, as in the case of issuing an income tax refund. The estimated receivable amount to be recognized is the refund amount. This is true with refunds being made from non-tax sources, as well.

According to the GASB Statement Number 38, receivables that are significant must be disclosed in the financial statement's notes. Also, receivables that are not going to be collected for at least one year should be disclosed. Disclosure, however, is not required when receivables are reported on the face of the government's financial statement.

Operating materials and supplies

Key rules for recording operating materials and supplies using the consumption method include:
- Operating materials and supplies are assets which are recognized as they are received.
- To value the cost of materials consumed, a flow assumption is required. However, federal agencies are prohibited from using the last in, first out (LIFO) flow assumption.
- The different categories of operating materials and supplies must be disclosed.

- Using the consumption method for recording operating materials and supplies, the following costs are to be recognized:
  - All historical costs
  - Costs associated with the delivery of operating materials and supplies
  - Costs incurred for improving the condition of operating materials and supplies.

Seized property

During the course of law enforcement activities, private property is sometimes seized, becoming the federal government's property. Types of property seized include physical personal property, currency, monetary instruments, and real property. The seized property is recorded at fair market value as an asset; however, a liability of the same amount must also be recorded since the federal government or agency is not allowed to use the property until it has been forfeited in a forfeiture proceeding. Property that is forfeited is done so to remove a tax lien or some other type of debt owed to the government. Abandoned or unclaimed property also becomes forfeited property. Once currency and monetary instruments are officially forfeited, the funds are reclassified on the balance sheet. They are shown as revenue since they are then available for the government's use, and the liability account is removed. Real and personal physical property is recognized at fair market value at the time of its forfeiture, as well. For all seized property except currency and monetary instruments, disclosure is required.

Capital assets

Capital assets classifications:
- *Machinery and Equipment:* This category encompasses a large range of items from phones to computers to cars. The value that should be recorded for these types of items should include: purchase price (net of trade-in allowances), delivery charges, and installation fees. Any additional costs necessary for preparing the item for its intended use may also be included.
- *Artwork and Historical Treasures:* When these items are donated, they should be recorded at their historical cost as a long-term investment. Although it is not required, the item should be capitalized if it is kept for a reason other than financial gains.
- *Infrastructure:* This category is for capital assets with a long useful life, such as roads and bridges.
- *Construction in Progress:* This is a temporary classification for capital asset projects during their construction phase. The construction costs include materials, direct labor, and overhead costs. Upon completion of the project, the costs are reclassified into an appropriate asset classification.

Additions, betterments, and preservations of capital assets

The purpose of additions and betterments is to extend the useful life of a capital asset, whereas preservation refers to the restoration of a capital asset. A government's capitalization policies dictate how costs are to be expensed. Typically, the costs of restoring a capital asset after it has been damaged are expensed as repair costs or maintenance costs. If a capital asset is not only restored but also improved upon, only the cost of the betterment may be capitalized. The cost of the betterment would be the additional cost beyond the point of restoration.

Impaired capital asset

An impaired capital asset is one that has unexpectedly had its useful life greatly reduced, such as by fire or tornado. If the government decides not to restore the impaired asset, the asset should be reported at the lower range of its fair market value. If the government does restore it back to its original condition, the costs of doing so should be reported. Money received from insurance claims should be reported separately.

Costs which should be included in each of the following capital asset classifications:

- *Land:* The total cost of the land should be recorded. These fees should be added to the purchase price to determine the total cost of land: survey, appraisal, title search, title transfer, and lawyer fees. If any additional costs were incurred to prepare the land for its intended use, such as tree removal costs, they should also be calculated into the total cost.
- *Buildings:* This category refers to permanent structures and their fixtures. Fixtures are attachments to the structure, such as attached cabinets, light fixtures, built-in bookcases, and mantles. The building's total cost should include: purchase price, contract fees, job order costs, architect costs, lawyer fees, and appraisal fees. Also any additional expenses incurred for making the building ready for its intended use may be added into the total cost.
- *Improvements:* All land improvements, except buildings, are recorded in this category. Examples include the costs of landscaping and creating walkways.

While most capital assets have a predetermined useful life over which their depreciation is expensed, some capital assets have a perpetual life, such as land; and so they are not depreciated. Infrastructure assets are capital assets with extremely long useful lives, such as roads. These assets are not depreciated when the government uses the modified asset approach, which declares the assets to be in better-than-average condition.

A government must disclose the capitalization policies it has adopted. This means it should disclose information regarding the sales, dispositions, and acquisitions of capital assets; the beginning and ending balances of capital assets; the accumulated depreciation; and current depreciation expenses reported by function.

Deferred revenue

Revenue that is owed to the government but not yet received by the government is called deferred revenue. For example, suppose an annual assessment tax is collected by the government. After the bill is issued, the amount due is considered deferred revenue. Issuance of the bill would be recorded by debiting Accounts Receivable and crediting Assessment Tax Revenue. To show that the revenue has not yet been received, Deferred Revenue becomes credited, and Assessment Tax Revenue is debited. The net result of these two journal entries shows a debit to Accounts Receivable and a credit to Deferred Revenue.

Compensated absences

Compensated absences for employees refers to the days that employees do not work but are still paid for it. Allowable absences may include: sick days, vacation time, and personal leaves of absences. Compensated days usually have to be earned. For example, one vacation day may be earned for every thirty days worked. Since it is expected that employees will take vacation and personal time, the government may be certain of this debt. Therefore, as compensated days accrue, the government must account for them as long-term liabilities. However, because sick days may or may not be used, they are not considered to be liabilities.

Reconciling transactions

Reconciling transactions between the fund level and the government-wide level for reporting:
- *Issuance of Long-term Debt*: The cash flow received from issuing long-term debt is shown on the Statement of Operations. The debt issuance is accounted for by crediting OFS – Proceeds from Debt Issuance and debiting Cash. To report it at the government-wide level, the following reconciling transaction must be recorded: OFS – Proceeds from Debt Issuance is debited and Long-term Debt is credited.
- *Retirement of Long-term Debt:* As the principal on long-term debt is repaid, it is accounted for using an entry that debits Debt Service Expenditure and credits Cash. The reconciling transaction used for reporting a decrease in liability at the government-wide level shows a debit to Retired Principal on Long-term Debt and a credit to Debt Service Expenditure. This liability reduction has no bearing on the Statement of Operations.

<u>Reconciliations that must take place between the fund level and the government-wide level for reporting:</u>

- *Capital Assets:* Assets costing more than a predetermined amount, known as the capitalization threshold, should be capitalized. At the fund level, capital assets are recorded by debiting Capital Outlay and crediting Cash. The reconciling transaction used for recording at the government-wide level debits Capital Assets and credits Capital Outlay.
- *Deferred Revenue:* At the fund level, earned revenue that is not readily available is reported as deferred revenue. At the government-wide level, all earned revenue is recognized and only unearned revenue is considered deferred. Therefore a reversing accounting entry must be made so that the fund-level's earned revenue that has been recorded as deferred revenue is recognized as revenue at the government-wide level.
- *Internal Service Funds:* At the fund level, internal service funds are classified as proprietary funds. If they predominantly service governmental funds, their assets and liabilities are classified at the government-wide level as governmental activities.

Reporting investment income

Investment income is reported as it accrues using the following accounting methods:
- *Accrual Basis of Accounting:* Investment income is recognized when it is earned.
- *Modified Accrual Basis of Accounting:* Investment income is recognized when it is available for spending.

For a governmental fund to record a loan it has made, the loan amount is debited in Expenditures for Loans and credited in Cash. Assuming repayment is expected, another entry must be made, debiting Loans Receivable and crediting Deferred Credit. The reason a deferred credit account is established is because repayment will not begin in the current period. When a loan payment is received, Cash is debited while both the Principal Payment Account and Interest Payment Account are credited for the amounts allocated to them. Finally a reversing entry, which debits Deferred Credit and credits Loans Receivable, must be made to correctly depict the outstanding loan amount.

Depreciation and straight-line method

For reporting purposes, assets with useful lives of one year or greater should be capitalized on either the Balance Sheet or Statement of Net Assets. Being capitalized simply means the amount paid for the asset is not expensed all at once when the purchase is recorded. Instead, the useful life of the asset is considered, and only the amount of the asset that is used or consumed during the accounting period is expensed. The expensed amount depreciates the asset's value and is known as depreciation. Proprietary and fiduciary funds report depreciation on their Operating Statements. Also it is seen on the Statement of Net Assets.

While there are various methods of calculating depreciation expense, most governments follow the Straight-line method. This method assumes the asset will be used or consumed equally for each year of its useful life. The Straight-line method uses the following formula to calculate an asset's yearly depreciation:

Asset value / Number of useful years = Annual depreciation

Intragovernmental amounts and segment information

Intragovernmental amounts refer to the values of two or more federal agencies and are included in the governmental-wide financial statements. The Office of Management and Budget requires federal agencies, not their component units, to report intragovernmental amounts in the required supplementary information, which is subject to audit. More specifically, it is the trade transactions involving assets, liabilities, non-exchange revenue, and earned revenue that must be reported as required supplementary information.

Segment information refers to the following fund information that has not been reported on government or agency's main financial statements: franchise funds and revolving funds used for intragovernmental support. As part of the required supplementary information, the segment information reports: condensed assets, liabilities, the fund's balance, accounts receivables, deferred revenues, a listing of major account classes, a summary of the services provided by the fund, the users of those services, and the gross and net costs of those services and goods.

Fund balance with the Treasury

The *fund balance with the Treasury* refers to the amount held by the Treasury on behalf of a government or agency to be used for its obligations, expenditures, or liabilities. This amount is recorded as an intragovernmental asset on the government/agency's accounting records and as an intragovernmental liability on the Treasury's recordkeeping. Appropriations, reappropriations, allocations, inward transfers, reimbursements, continuing resolutions, offsetting collections, and loans from the Treasury will inflate the fund balance with the Treasury. Payments towards liabilities, asset purchases, U.S. security investments, as well as, outward transfers, the cancellation of expired appropriations, sequestered appropriations, and rescinded appropriations will all reduce the fund balance with the Treasury.

Appropriation accounting

The purpose of appropriations is to limit and control government spending. In the federal government, Congress passes appropriations, and the president signs the appropriation bill, making it a law. At the state level, an appropriation bill is passed

- 57 -

by a state legislature, and the governor signs it into law. Finally, local governments have city councils who legislate appropriations. The accounting of appropriations is necessary, as governments must submit a required report regarding the status of their appropriations. The status should include adjustments, encumbrances, expenditures, and obligations. Thus, appropriation accounting maintains accountability over the amount and ways revenues are spent.

Budgeting

Purposes

While there are no official standards for the budgetary process in governments, and it often changes as new public leaders take office; it is still necessary for budgets to be created in all levels of government. Budgets are needed for determining what resources are available, how those resources should be allocated among the programs, and thus they ultimately determine what services will be available to the public.

NACSLB

To help governments make their budgets, a National Advisory Council on State and Local Budgets (NACSLB) was established, and in 1998 they created guidelines called the "Recommended Budget Practices – A Framework for Improved State and Local Government Budgeting". The guidelines encourage governments to consider their long-term needs, to make general objectives, and to ensure budget decisions are correctly conveyed to the appropriate people. The NACSLB also suggests providing incentives to encourage employees for finding ways to improve the budgetary process.

Central Budget Authority

The Central Budget Authority creates and enforces policies and procedures regarding budgetary spending. It is independently staffed from all other programs or services so as to remain unbiased. To achieve its main purpose of ensuring internal controls over budgetary spending are effective and efficient, the Central Budget Authority monitors the performance of programs and services. It reviews their stated goals and estimated revenues and compares them to actual goals and revenues. When revenues are lower than expected, the Central Budgetary Authority has the duty of creating and implementing corrective procedures.

Agency budgetary controls are more extensive than the Central Budgetary Authority's controls. They are created by larger government agencies, are more detailed, and are mostly directed towards an agency's individual programs and the reporting of monthly and quarterly results, in addition to, comparisons of estimated and actual results. There must be good communication between an agency issuing agency budgetary controls and the Central Budgetary Authority issuing centralized budgetary controls for efforts to be coordinated in establishing and implementing effective and efficient budgetary controls.

Process

Preparation phase

The budgetary process begins with the preparation phase. The first step in that phase is to have the government leader, such as the mayor of a city or the Governor of a state, document the government's long-term plans and state its main objectives. The Chief Financial Officer (CFO) reviews the objectives from which he creates a budget calendar which provides details of which people are required to do the specified tasks by the stated dates in order for established goals to be met. The CFO also makes economic predictions and financial projections by analyzing historical financial data and comparing it to current data. The main objectives, budget calendar, and other related information are reviewed with relevant parties so their feedback may be taken into account. A budget request is then sent to the appropriate legislative body.

Legislative phase

Once a legislative body receives a budget request, public hearings are held, allowing affected parties of the general public to comment on the proposed budget and to offer suggestions. In the federal government, members of the Senate and House of Representatives review the budget request. A committee is formed to incorporate viable suggestions and refine the budget until both the Senate and House agree on it. This mutual agreement is necessary for the budget to be officially adopted. If the House and Senate cannot agree on the proposed budget, a Continuing Resolution must be passed. This allows the government to continue its day-to-day operations while they work on a compromise. If they reach a stalemate and neither legislative body is willing to compromise, the government will be forced to cease operations until proper authority is given for them to resume. Although local governments have only a single legislative body, their legislative phase resembles that of the federal government's.

Budget execution phase

Approval of the proposed budget or appropriation bill by both the Senate and House of Representatives marks the beginning of the budget execution phase. The budget bill is then enacted. As a law, the budget dictates the appropriation of revenues among the various governments and government agencies. There is some flexibility in the budget, however, which allows a government or agency to transfer a limited percentage of its appropriated funds to another government or agency.

Once governments receive their allotted revenues, it should be noted that the spending of those funds depends on the procedures and policies of the respective governments. Any amendments to the budget take place during this phase.

Information in government budgets

Government budgets should contain the following information to help identify exactly where resources are allocated and where funds are being spent:
- *Organizational Unit*: This identifies the government agency, such as the Department of Motor Vehicles.
- *Function:* This specifies which services or programs are offered by the agency. For example, a function of the DMV would be its Driver's licensing service.
- *Program:* This breaks down the service or program by the individual tasks and activities it does. For example the driver's licensing service produces a driver's handbook, tests drivers, and issues them licenses.
- *Category:* This classifies revenues and expenses by their source. Examples include: tax revenue, user fee revenue, or employee wage expense.
- *Line Item or Object:* This refers to specific expenses.

Approaches

The following are types of budgeting approaches:
- *Line item budgeting approach*: Budget request is made for each line item contained in the budget. A specific amount is determined for each individual line item. This figure indicates the highest allowable amount of money that may be spent towards that item. This type of approach helps control spending and is commonly used by state and local governments.
- *Program budgeting approach:* Does not concern itself with the expense of individual line items, but rather it focuses on the cost of the entire program. This approach allows for more flexibility with regard to how the funds within a program are spent. Also, it is easy for users of the program budget report to know the exact amount of funding each program received.
- *Zero-base budgeting approach:* Starts all government agencies with zero dollars in their budget. Various levels of management must create budget proposals for the different programs and services offered by the agency. They are expected to justify the programs and services they want to continue or add by pointing out the benefits of them, as well as, explaining the consequences that would result if the services or programs were dropped. An agency's budget is increased with each program or service that can be adequately justified. Since this budgeting approach requires a great deal of time and money, it is not a preferable method.
- *Performance budgeting approach:* Interested in the amount of outputs or the quality of the outcome that can be achieved from a certain amount of resources. Since this method views outputs to inputs, or outcomes to resources, it allows the user to easily determine ways to improve efficiency. The Government Accountability Office published guidelines for using this approach, called the Government Performance and Results Act.

- *Baseline budgeting approach:* A budget that is being prepared for the next fiscal year is created based on the current fiscal year's figures. This type of approach is used as a starting point for estimating the next year's costs for providing the same programs and services. Naturally changes will occur, however, in the next year; some programs or services will be dropped, changed, or added, and so the budget would have to be altered accordingly.

Capital budgets

In addition to the operating budget, governments also create a capital budget which reveals sources of income, borrowed funds, and plans for capital improvements or projects. State and local governments submit these budges separately. The operating budget represents the government's day-to-day needs, as opposed to the capital budget which refers to their wants. Therefore, when resources are tight, the capital budget receives less attention, as capital projects are postponed. When there is available funding, the capital budget is more carefully reviewed.

The federal government presents the operating and capital budgets simultaneously. Its capital budget, however, must have justification for the outlaying of funds, and it should propose other methods and means by which the project goals may be met.

Funding capital projects

If current tax revenues are tight, a government may finance a capital project by:
- *Charging an Assessment Tax:* First the government sells assessment bonds and uses the proceeds to fund the project. Anyone using or benefiting from the completed project is charged an assessment tax. The government uses these revenues to pay the principal and interest on the assessment bonds.
- *Receiving Intergovernmental Grants:* The federal and state governments set aside some of their revenues to offer grants to local governments.
- *Issuing Bonds or Notes:* Since governments have many restrictions on the funding of capital projects, financing authorities have been created to oversee debt issuances and to ensure they comply with restrictions. An example of a restriction is the length in time a state or local government may allow revenue from a bond issue to sit idle; to be in compliance, governments must coordinate the issuance with the project's spending schedule. Upon project completion, the outstanding debt securities should not exceed the project's cost, and their maturity dates may not exceed the project's useful life.

Revenue forecasting techniques

Revenue forecasting techniques used by federal, state, and local governments include:
- *Historical Data*: After many years of receiving revenues form the same source, the historical data may be statistically analyzed to predict future revenues.
- *Revenue Growth Rates*: Calculations of future revenues may be based on an average annual growth rate. However modifications may be necessary to reflect any major economic changes.
- *Cost-Benefit Analysis*: This compares costs to benefits. The greater the benefits are in relation to costs, the greater value the program or service holds.
- *Regression Analysis*: This statistically determines the relationship between variables so that future values may be forecasted.
- *Net Present Value (NPV)*: This technique determines the present value of future cash inflows and then subtracts the initial costs to arrive at the net present value.

Budgetary terms

To prevent a budget deficit, government spending must be controlled so that it does not exceed revenues. One method to help control spending is to divide an original allocation of funds into smaller amounts to be used during designated time periods of the fiscal year or for certain specific goals. In the federal government, this method is known as *apportionment*. The federal government's Office of Management and Budgets determines and controls apportionments. This same method is used by local and state governments, but it is known as *allotment*.

Funds that have already been promised to other parties through contracts or other binding agreements must be taken out of the initial appropriation and set aside to ensure they will be available when payments are due. These promised funds are known as *obligations* in the federal government and called *encumbrances* in state and local governments.

Budgetary comparison schedule

A budgetary comparison schedule shows the estimated budget with the actual budget, and although it is not required, the difference between the two amounts is commonly included, as well. The planned budget should include amounts that were carried over from the previous year while the final actual budget should include the following information: the estimated budget amounts, as well as, transfers, supplemental appropriations, and other changes that altered the original estimated amounts. If the budget was created without following GAAP, reconciliation between the budgetary comparison schedule and the Operating Statement, which does follow GAAP, is required.

All general funds and major special revenue funds are required to have a budgetary comparison schedule accompany their financial statements as supplemental information. Funds that do not require a budgetary comparison schedule include: debt service, major capital project, enterprise, and permanent funds.

Intergovernmental grants

Intergovernmental grants are gifts of money, assets, or other resources from one government or non-profit organization/foundation awarded to another government, usually with stipulations from the grantor on how the resources are to be used.

Types of intergovernmental grants include:
- *Capital Grants:* A grant that is designated to be used strictly for acquiring or constructing capital assets.
- *Operating Grants:* A grant meant to be spent on operations and/or capital expenditures. Typically the recipient of the grant is allowed to choose how to allocate the gifted resources.
- *Pass-through Grant:* A grant awarded to a government that is expected to award the grant to another party.

Grant classifications include:
- *Categorical Grants:* Grants designated for a specific purpose or program.
- *Block Grants:* Grants with few or no restrictions, allowing its resources to be spent for a broad range of purposes or programs.
- *Formula Grants:* The amount awarded to a recipient in this type of grant is based on a formula that takes into account relevant factors, such as the average age or income of a potential recipient's population.
- *Discretionary Grants:* These types of grants must be applied for by filling out an application. The grantor reviews the applications and then awards grant funds as he sees fit.

In order to recognize grant revenues, the following eligibility requirements must be met:
- The grant must be received by a party who matches all the eligibility requirements set forth by the grantor. For example, a law enforcement agency would be eligible to receive a grant for handguns whereas a public school system would not be eligible.
- The recipient spends the grant money within the specified time limit as set forth by the grantor. If grant money is spent before or after the specified time constraints, that amount is ineligible.

- The grantor clearly defines which resources, if any, may be reimbursed for their usage.
- If the grantor has contingencies, they are clearly defined.

Budgetary resources

Budgetary resources are the resources available for: immediate spending or for commitment to contractual obligations requiring payment during a specified time period. These resources include borrowing authority, contract authority, spending authority for offsetting collections, the current year's appropriated funds, unobligated balances from multi-year and no-year appropriations, and any recoveries from prior years' obligations. Budgetary resources must be available prior to being spent or otherwise obligated. The status of budgetary resources shows them as: obligations incurred, unobligated balances that are available, and unobligated balances that are unavailable. Unobligated balances that are unavailable may be unavailable due to the termination in budgetary authority or an expired appropriation. The status of budgetary resources is always equal to the amount of budgetary resources, as it merely classifies them. For accurate budgeting, it is imperative that transactions are charged to the proper appropriation. For example, funds are to be considered obligated and charged to the current appropriation at the time a good/service is ordered, not to the appropriation during the time the good/service is used or when payment is sent.

Statement of Budgetary Resources

The purpose of the Statement of Budgetary Resources is to report information regarding the sources, allocation, and spending of budgetary resources. It should show the amount of resources remaining and the obligations incurred by the end of the period. It is interesting to note that while other financial statements are reporting information from the financial accounting system, the Statement of Budgetary Resources relies on the budget accounting system for its information regarding the allocations and expenses/expenditures of budgetary resources. Important information is included in the statement's budget execution, and is therefore subject to being audited. The rules for preparing a Statement of Budgetary Resources may be found in the Report on Budget Execution and Budgetary Resources.

The amounts reported in the Statement of Budgetary Resources are cumulative. These cumulative amounts should be segregated by individual major budget accounts in the required supplementary information (RSI). The small accounts may be reported in aggregate. The total of the accounts reported in the required supplementary information should match the cumulative figures given in the Statement of Budgetary Resources.

It is mandatory for all deferred maintenance to be reported in the required supplementary information. It should include the following details: the major asset class to which the deferred maintenance belongs; the method of measurement, either life cycle method or condition assessment method; and its dollar value.

Total budgetary resources

The Statement of Budgetary Resources begins with the *budget authority*. Then the *unobligated balance* is given for the start of the fiscal year. *Net transfers* are reported and used to show the *actual unobligated balance*.

The *spending authority from offsetting collections* is addressed next by listing the earned offsetting collections that are received from federal sources. Then *changes in unfilled customer orders* report advances received and those without advances from federal sources to arrive at the *subtotal spending from offsetting collections*. Next, *recoveries of prior year obligations, resources temporarily not available*, and *resources permanently not available* are reported and used to determine the amount to report for the *total budgetary resources*.

After the first portion of *total budgetary resources*, the next major section in the Statement of Budgetary Resources deals with the status of budgetary resources. It begins by listing the direct and the reimbursable obligations incurred and totaling them. Then the amount of the unobligated balance that is apportioned and the amount that is exempt from apportionment is shown. Following that is the unobligated balances not available. The combined result of the obligations incurred, the unobligated balance, and the unobligated balance not available determines the total status of budgetary resources.

The next section shows the "Total Unpaid Obligated Balance, Net, End of Fiscal Year" by starting with the unpaid obligated balance and adjusting it for such things as gross outlays and balance transfers.

The final section covers Net Outlays. Gross outlays are reduced by *offsetting collections* and further reduced by *distributed offsetting receipts*, thus totaling Net Outlays.

- 66 -

State and Local Financial Accounting and Reporting

Primary government criteria

A state or local government must meet the following criteria to be considered a *primary government.* It must be a legally separate entity which holds its own elections and maintains financial independence from all other state and local governments. Financial independence in this sense is defined as the ability to: levy taxes, determine taxing rates, issue debt obligations, set fees, as well as, create, enact, and adjust a budget without another government's approval.

A *special purpose government* may be a primary government if it meets the qualifications in the definition of a primary government. A special purpose government, however, is subject to being overseen by a separate governing body.

COP's and level debt service

With certificates of participation (COP's), an investor is buying a portion of the revenues which will be received from a particular government lease. For example, the government may lease purchase an asset. The party they are buying the asset from sells shares of the lease purchase agreement to investors. These shares are known as certificates of participation. The title to the leased asset is held by a trustee. The government makes payments to the trustee who then passes them on to the certificate holders.

A level debt service simply means the government's debt on the bond issue is amortized so that even though different amounts of principal and interest are being paid each year, the total payment remains fairly constant throughout the life of the bond issue. This is similar to how a homeowner pays his mortgage debt. Governments like a level debt service because it is easy to budget.

Landfills

EPA and landfill accounting
In 1993, the Environmental Protection Agency (EPA) made new regulations stating that all landfills must be monitored during and after closure, including those previously closed. To comply with these regulations, governments typically pay the costs of closing and monitoring a closed landfill over a twenty to fifty year period. As a result, governments must now report landfills as long-term debt obligations. This requires estimating their future costs, which is difficult since these costs encompass unknown variables, such as inflation and future EPA restrictions, which are not easily predictable. To assist in the accounting of landfills, following the 1993 regulations, the Governmental Accounting Standards Board (GASB) issued guidelines.

- 67 -

<u>Closing and post-closing costs for landfills</u>
Generally Accepted Accounting Principles (GAAP) state that all of the estimated closing and post-closing costs of a landfill should be recognized while a landfill is still in use despite the fact that cash outlays may not directly correlate. This is accomplished by expensing a portion of the total estimated closing and post-closing costs over the landfill's active life so that when it does close, all the costs have been recognized. These costs are reported as operating or capital expenses. As they are paid, the correlating accumulated liability is reduced by the same amount. If the actual expense turns out to be greater than the estimated cost, the account is classified as a net pre-paid account. When the actual expense is less than the estimated cost, the account is classified as a liability.

Operating versus capital leases

The lease agreements used for acquiring fixed assets are considered to be either operating leases or capital leases and should be capitalized at the start of the lease. The lease is reported as an operating lease unless certain conditions exist, in which case it is reported as a capital lease. The conditions which determine if a lease agreement is a capital lease are as follows:
- It is written in the lease that the property will transfer ownership to the lessee by the lease's end.
- The lease has an "option to buy" clause built into the agreement.
- The term of the lease agreement lasts for 75% of the property's useful life, or longer.
- The lease payment's present value is 90% of the property's fair value, or higher.

Property escheatment

Property escheatment refers to a property's ownership being reverted to a government. There are various circumstances in which this may happen.

Example 1: A deposit was made to a government utility and never claimed. Accounting Records – The government records unclaimed deposits as revenue to a governmental or proprietary fund and accounts for any amount that may be refundable as a liability.

Example 2: A citizen, who has no will or heirs, dies. Accounting Records – Property that had been privately owned, by a citizen or other non-governmental entity, must be reported in a private-purpose trust fund or an agency fund.

Example 3: A decorative wood bench is found on the roadside with no identification. After several months of it not being claimed, the city places it in their park for public use. Accounting Records – If the government chooses to allow escheated property to be used publicly, it must create a liability account for the value of the property that could be claimed.

Governmental fund operating statements

The timing of when revenues are recognized on governmental fund operating statements is based on when they are both measurable and available. To be considered available, the revenue must be received and available for spending in the current fiscal period. Revenue that is not available is recorded as deferred revenue.

Proprietary funds categorize all of their revenues as either operating or non-operating revenue. If the revenues are received due to an exchange of government-provided goods or services, they are considered operating revenues. If the revenues are due to other transactions, such as from selling capital assets, they are reported as non-operating revenue.

Capital outlays

Obtaining or constructing a capital asset requires capital outlays, which are recorded as expenditures. Such a transaction shows a credit to Cash and a debit to Expenditures–Capital Outlay. In cases of large capital construction projects, it is common for a government to withhold a portion of the contractor's payment. This withheld portion is referred to as retainage and does not have any bearing on the amount recorded as a capital outlay expenditure. The purpose of the retainage is to ensure the contractor completes the construction as agreed upon. After he does, the retainage is released to him. It should be noted that a reconciliation of capital outlays between the fund-level and the government-wide financial statements is necessary.

Principal payments to long-term debt

Current financial assets or other current resources are used to reduce the principal balance owed on long-term debt. The transaction is recorded on the Operating Statement unless payments on principal are made in proprietary or fiduciary funds, in which case those payments are not recorded in the Operating Statement. Reconciliation is necessary between the fund-level and governmental-wide financial statements since principal payments made toward long-term debt are not reported on the government-wide Statement of Activities. Costs that should be reported as debt issuance costs on the Operating Statement may include: underwriting fees, lawyer fees, as well as, the production and distribution costs of the prospectuses.

Federal Financial Accounting and Reporting

Accounting systems

Federal, state, and local governments use both budgetary and proprietary/financial accounting systems, as each one serves its own unique purpose.

A budgetary accounting system focuses on future expenditures, and thus it is used as a tool for controlling government spending. It shows a starting balance for the fiscal year, the amount of funds already obligated to certain areas or projects, and finally the remaining available funds. Using the budgetary system, an appropriate allocation of the remaining available funds must be determined.

A proprietary/financial accounting system reports on the past year's expenditures, showing a financial record of the year's projects, programs, and events. The data is necessary for assessing a government's performance and determining its progress over the year. Financial statements are produced from this type of accounting system, and so the system must be periodically audited.

Cash basis vs. accrual basis of accounting

Accounting on a *cash basis* means entries are made when cash is physically moved. It is recorded on the date received and the date paid out. While this method of accounting is simple, many have argued that it does not provide a true representation of an institution's financial state. For example, an entity may have received assets that it has not yet been billed for, or it may have sent goods to consumers and not yet received payment for those goods.

An *accrual basis* of accounting corrects this inaccuracy by recording cash when it is earned, not necessarily received, and when an expense is incurred, not necessarily paid. Under this method, prepaid expenses are recorded as assets until the expense is truly incurred, and the depreciation of capital property and equipment is expensed over their useful lives.

Budgetary versus proprietary accounting

The main objective of budgetary accounting is to monitor and control resource allocation, capital outlays, and receipts while the main concern in proprietary accounting is the financial outcome resulting from governmental operations. Budgetary journal entries match expenditures to the correct appropriation; in other words, expenditures are charged to the current appropriation at the time the goods are received, regardless of when they are used or when payment for them is sent. Proprietary entries, on the other hand, expense goods/services as they are consumed or used. Also, proprietary entries are concerned with accurately recording long-term assets (assets with a useful life greater than one year).

The following situations would require a budgetary accounting journal entry but not a proprietary accounting entry:

- *Situation A:* Once a commitment to pay for needed goods/services has been secured, the following budgetary entry is made even though no exchange has taken place: Realized Resources is debited and Commitments is credited. This situation would not need a proprietary journal entry.
- *Situation B:* Once the goods/services have been ordered from an outside vendor but not yet received, the obligation of funds would be recognized in this budgetary accounting entry: Commitments would be debited and Undelivered Orders would be credited. This situation would not be recognized in proprietary accounting.

The following situations would require a proprietary accounting journal entry but not a budgetary accounting journal entry:

- *Situation A*: A federal agency submits its disbursement schedule to the Department of Treasury so the Treasury will issue payments towards the agency's obligations. Proprietary accounting would record this action by: debiting Accounts Payable and crediting Disbursements in Transit. Budgetary accounting would not make a journal entry.
- *Situation B:* Once the Department of Treasury issues checks for the agency's obligations, a proprietary accounting journal entry is made, debiting Disbursements in Transit and crediting Fund Balance with Department of Treasury. Budgetary accounting does not record this.
- *Situation C:* The federal agency consumes goods. A proprietary accounting record shows the consumption of goods by debiting Operating Expenses and crediting Supplies. This is not recorded in budgetary accounting.

Accounting entries

When a new fiscal year begins, expected revenues for the year are estimated and recorded in a budget, along with expected appropriations. If the estimated revenues and appropriations are equal in amount, there is no need for a journal entry. If expected revenues exceed budgeted appropriations, *appropriations* are credited and *estimated revenues* are debited. If the reverse happens (more appropriations than anticipated revenues), *appropriations* are still credited and *estimated revenues* are still debited; however, the *budgetary fund balance* must also be adjusted with a debit. If a supplemental appropriation needs to be made during the year, it should be recorded as follows: the budgetary fund balance is debited, and the appropriation is credited.

To record encumbrances, which are funds set aside for a specific purpose, the encumbrances account is debited and the reserve for encumbrances account is

- 71 -

credited. As these funds are spent on the specific purpose and the good/service is received, one journal entry should show *reserve for encumbrances* debited and *encumbrances* credited; a second journal must debit the appropriate expense account and credit the vouchers payable account.

Interim revenue and expenditure reporting

Partway through the year, interim revenue reporting is done to determine unrealized revenues by comparing actual revenues to estimated revenues. Based on the results, it may be decided that the original estimate of revenues was too high. To lower the amount of estimated revenues in the accounting records, *estimated revenues* should be credited and the *budgetary fund balance* should be debited. However, if actual revenues are proving to be better than expected, the estimate may be increased by debiting *estimated revenues* and crediting the *budgetary fund balance.*

Interim expenditure reports are prepared during the year to determine the availability of funds that may be used for spending. Available funds are calculated as follows: appropriations minus expenditures and encumbrances.

Revenue classifications

Federal agencies classify their revenues as either Receipts or Offsetting Collection/Receipts, depending on the type of activities which brought the inflow of funds.

- *Receipts:* If the revenue-inducing activity relates to a governing power, such as taxation, tariffs, and licensing fees; the revenue is recorded as a Receipt. Finding the difference between receipts and net outlays will show the resulting surplus or deficit.
- *Offsetting Collections/Receipts:* If revenue is obtained from business-type activities, it is reported as an Offsetting Collections/Receipt. This includes such transactions with the public as collecting an admission to a state park or receiving revenues from gift shop sales at an historic site. It also includes intergovernmental transactions, whereby revenue is received from another government in exchange for goods/services rendered. Offsetting Collections/Receipts are subtracted from gross outlays to determine net outlays.

Recording expended authority

After the delivery of ordered goods is received, the federal agency makes the following entry: a debit to Undelivered Orders and a credit to Allotments – Realized Resources, as well as, a credit to Expended Authority. Supposing at the time of delivery the actual cost was less than the estimated cost, the Allotment account balance would be increased by the difference between the estimated and actual

- 72 -

costs while the Expended Authority account would reflect the actual cost. This journal entry, made at the time of delivery, removes the payment obligation from the books despite the fact that the vendor has not actually received payment. This happens because the obligation is no longer a concern to the federal agency because the agency periodically submits a disbursement schedule to the Department of Treasury, as it is the Treasury's responsibility to issue payments to vendors.

Closing entries

At the end of the fiscal year, appropriations are no longer available for spending and all revenue has been realized. Closing entries must be made to the budgetary accounting records. Closing the estimated revenues and appropriations accounts, requires debiting the appropriations account, debiting the budgetary fund accounts, and crediting the estimated revenues account so that their balances are zero. Encumbrance accounts can be either closed, in which case a new appropriation is determined for the next fiscal year, or they may be extended into the new fiscal year. In the latter case, the encumbrance account's outstanding balance is equivalent to a predetermined amount that is reserved from the fund's balance.

U.S. government's budget

The federal budget of the United States government, or president's budget, is planned eighteen months prior to the beginning of its fiscal year. The federal government's fiscal year begins October 1 and finishes on September 30. The budget takes into account the president's recommendations, including suggested resource allocations and noted priorities. Congress determines appropriations for all of its budgets; these amounts should not only be based on the current fiscal year's needs but should also consider the next four years. The budget should include the previous year's actual budget amounts to serve as a comparison.

Budgetary policies

The U.S. president begins drafting the federal budget by creating budgetary policies, which are then given to the Office of Management and Budgets (OMB) to be further developed. The OMB also receives budget requests from government agencies. These requests are reviewed by analysts. Any concerns are reported to the OMB for their further discussion with the specific government agencies. Appropriate officials from each of the branches of government are also invited to collaborate with the president and the director of the OMB to finalize the policies that will be used for the current fiscal year and the four fiscal years there after. The same individuals stay in contact to discuss additional proposals, new information, and assessments that may have a bearing on the proposed policies. Factors that are taken into consideration during the policy-making process include: interest rates, unemployment rates, inflation rates, economic forecasts, past budget performance, increases in the Gross Domestic Product, and the percentage of salaries/wages making up the Gross

Domestic Product. As agreements are reached over major issues, the drafting of the budget begins.

Securing funding

Federal agencies must have authorization to receive funding for a program or activity. First they should fulfill Congress' requirements for establishing a federal program or activity, as it is up to Congress to decide whether or not to grant authorization for funding. Obtaining authorization does not mean the agency may immediately start spending or incurring debt, other than in a few exceptional circumstances. It simply means they have been approved to receive an appropriation. Congress makes sure the appropriated funds received by an agency correctly match the agency's expected expenditures, and that the expenditures have a reasonable purpose. Congress also ensures federal agencies only spend and incur debt to their allowable limits and during their specified time period.

Appropriation life cycle

The life cycle of an appropriation is completed in six or more years. The life cycle's periods are as follows:
- *Current Period:* The current period lasts one year for an annual appropriation, for the legally specified time period for multiple-year appropriations, and indefinitely for no-year appropriations. In the current period, the total available funding which may be allocated towards new programs and obligations is calculated.
- *Expired Period:* Any unused amounts of funds from appropriations that have expired at the end of the fiscal year may be used to pay off expenditures that were incurred prior to the appropriation's expiration date, not after. These payments toward obligations should not exceed a 5-year period.
- *Closed Period:* After the five years, the appropriation is considered closed. No more payments may be made, and any remaining obligation is cancelled at this time.

Permanent laws

Permanent laws grant the following:
- *Appropriations:* Appropriations are legally obtained through approved appropriation bills. They allow government agencies to spend funds and incur debt.
- *Authority to Borrow:* This authority grants government agencies the ability to borrow from the general fund or U.S. Treasury in order to fulfill other financial obligations.
- *Contract Authority:* This type of authority gives government agencies permission to incur financial obligations before they receive their appropriation.

- *Spending Authority from Offsetting Collections:* This allows a government agency to incur financial obligations or spend funds from the Offsetting Collections account by crediting the account for the amount it uses and debiting that amount to an expenditure account.

Spending requirements

Federal government spending must comply with the provisions and requirements set forth by the U.S. Constitution. Under its Article I, Section 9, Clause 7, the only funds that may be withdrawn from the U.S. Treasury are those that have been appropriated. According to the Constitution, appropriations require congress' approval and must be named prior to any disbursal of their funds. Section 9 of Article I also states that government expenditures and receipts are required to be reported in financial statements that are publicly accessible. More specifically, the U.S. Treasury is expected to issue a Statement of Receipts and Outlays monthly. Financial provisions are granted to Congress in Article I, Section 8, Clause 2 of the Constitution. It states that Congress has the authority to use the credit of the United States to borrow funds.

Restrictions on government agencies

Government agencies are not allowed to spend money or incur debt obligations prior to receiving their appropriation. Once they receive their appropriation, they must be careful not to spend more than that amount, as over-spending is prohibited. These restrictions are enforced by the Anti-Deficiency Act. Also under the Anti-Deficiency Act, the executive branch, or more specifically the Office of Management and Budgets (OMB), is authorized to oversee the allocation of resources among government agencies which is typically done by time periods. If an agency or program needs additional funding during the year due to unforeseen circumstances, the president may prompt Congress to adjust the budget. While the president is prohibited from spending or retaining appropriations under the Impoundment Control Act of 1974, he may submit a deferral to congress suggesting that the expenditure of funds be delayed. This would take effect immediately if the deferral is not rejected by Congress. The president may also propose a rescission to revoke the budget authority already granted. Congress has forty-five days to approve the proposal by passing the necessary legislation; otherwise the rescission does not occur.

The Congressional Act of 1974

The Congressional Act of 1974 created Budget Committees from within the House of Representatives and the Senate. These committees have been granted the sole responsibility of focusing on the budget. This includes reporting an economic forecast, establishing the yearly budget resolution, monitoring all actions regarding the federal budget, and overseeing the operation of the Congressional Budget Office (CBO). Congress' authority over the budget includes being able to: approve, reject, or modify the president's budget proposal, cut or add programs, reduce or increase taxation, change funding amounts, and to extend spending authority to federal agencies. It should be noted that budgeted appropriations are not listed in one comprehensive bill but rather enacted through many bills.

Congressional actions

- *Budget Resolution:* This documents budget limits set by Congress. It contains definitive amounts for debt limits, total receipts, the total spending, and deficit/surplus levels. Congressional committees use it as a guide for creating appropriations bills.
- *Authorizing Legislation:* This type of legislation approves the continuation or start-up of a federal program or agency, and stipulates any restrictions it must follow, such as sanctions, obligations, and expenditures. It also authorizes funds to be spent on stated purposes.
- *Appropriation Bill:* The House of Representatives proposes appropriation bills, which seek the legal allocation of proposed funds. The Senate may accept or reject the bills.

Budget-related terms:

- *Conference Committees:* If the Senate disagrees with one of the House's appropriation bills, a conference committee works toward a resolution. The bill is then revised and reintroduced for the House and Senate's approval.
- *Presidential Approval:* An approved appropriations bill is sent to the president for his approval or veto.
- *Continuing Resolution:* If a budget has not been signed into law in time for the new fiscal year, a resolution grants authority to continue government operations by funding government agencies at current or reduced levels until a formal appropriations bill is signed.
- *Budget Authority:* This is the legal authority for a government or government agency to make appropriations, enter into contractual agreements, borrow funds, and spend funds.
- *Mandatory Spending:* This refers to required spending toward government programs for which the federal government has a legal obligation to finance. Examples of such programs include Medicare and Social Security.
- *Discretionary Spending:* This is defined as spending on government programs that the federal government is not legally obligated to finance. Such spending needs Congress' authorization. In a fiscal year, discretionary spending makes up about one-third of the federal government's total spending.
- *Treasury Warrants:* Government agencies receive their appropriations from the U.S. Treasury. They are issued as Treasury Warrants.

Title 31, Section 1301

Title 31 of the United States Code, Section 1301 gives direction on how appropriations are to be handled. It states that Congress is responsible for overseeing how appropriated funds are spent and ensuring they are spent according to their designated purposes. It further states that spending may not go towards any unauthorized items, and spending on authorized items must be charged to the correct appropriation. The code prohibits the transfer of funds between appropriations unless there is statuary authority for doing so.

Types of appropriations:
- *Definite Appropriation:* An appropriation with a limit on its amount.
- *Indefinite Appropriation:* The appropriated amount is dependent on an unknown variable, such as the program's number of eligible recipients, and therefore does not have a predetermined limit.

Anti-Deficiency Act

The Anti-Deficiency Act establishes the responsibilities of federal agencies regarding their appropriations. To ensure federal agencies do not spend over their appropriated amounts nor spend so quickly that their funds are used up before year-end, the Anti-Deficiency Act holds the federal agencies' heads accountable for creating policies to restrict expenditures and obligations. It further states that the agencies' heads are responsible for developing controls to detect violators of the Anti-Deficiency Act. The Act prohibits federal agencies from participating in the following activities:
- Acquiring goods/services prior to receiving its appropriation
- To enter into a contract which involves an amount greater than the lesser of either the current year's appropriation amount or the amount apportioned from the Office of Management and Budgets. (OMB)
- Accept offered services that were volunteered
- Issue payments from a depleted appropriation account

1990 Budget Enforcement Act

The Balanced Budget and Deficit Control Act of 1985, the Congressional Budget and Impoundment Control Act of 1974, and the Gramm-Rudman-Hollings Act were all amended in 1990 by the Budget Enforcement Act. The purpose of the Budget Enforcement Act is to better control federal spending. Under the Act, spending is grouped as either discretionary or mandatory. Since mandatory spending is required and often indefinite, it is controlled by budget authority, whereas discretionary spending is easily controlled through appropriations. Spending caps are placed on domestic, defense, and international discretionary spending. These caps are considered flexible for emergency situations. Finally, all receipts follow the rules of mandatory spending.

Federal Credit Reform Act of 1990

The federal programs that give direct loans or guarantee loans are controlled by the Federal Credit Reform Act of 1990. Under this act, the budgets of these programs have specific requirements on how to be handled. Subsidy costs from direct loans and the default risk on guaranteed loans must be carefully calculated, as the act requires that the program's subsidy costs serve as the allowed amount for which Congress may appropriate to them. The program is prohibited from giving loans and guarantees until it receives its appropriation. The act also calls for additional accounting standards to recognize direct loan disbursements and outstanding loans as assets. Meanwhile the outstanding guaranteed loan balances are to be shown as liabilities with the loans' face values and the net present value of their estimated cash flows being disclosed.

Supplemental Appropriation Act

The Supplemental Appropriation Act of 1950 identified the type of obligations that may be legally matched to appropriations. It also mandated that at the end of the fiscal year, governments and their agencies must report any liquidated and unobligated appropriations.

Government Performance Results Act

The Government Performance Results Act of 1993 was designed to have federal programs and agencies focus on accomplishing their goals. It requires performance plans with stated goals and objectives to be developed annually. Also annual performance reports must be issued, revealing if stated goals were attained and if so, to what extent. Financial reports and other required reporting should be included in the Performance and Accountability Report. According to the act, the Office of Management Budgets (OMB) should mainly base their decisions regarding appropriation requests on the requesting agency's or program's performance reports.

Office of Management and Budgets

The Office of Management and Budgets' (OMB) primary responsibilities include:
- Working with the U.S. President to create a federal budget
- Determining the federal budget's funding priorities
- Establishing and improving regulatory policies
- Serving as a board to oversee the financial management of government agencies and programs and their funding process
- Reviewing the budget and funding requests submitted by various federal agencies

- Ensuring Federal agency reports follow applicable rules and policies, including the president's budget and administrative policies
- Assessing the effectiveness and efficiency of programs based on their performance results
- Designing and implementing better performance measures
- Contributing to advancements in program management

U.S. Department of Treasury

The United States Department of Treasury is responsible for managing the federal government's finances, as well as, being the government's fiscal agent.

The *Financial Management Service* of the Department of Treasury is in charge of the following tasks:
- Disbursing federal government payments
- Collecting an annual amount of over $2 trillion
- Monitoring the government's everyday cash flow
- Maintaining a debt collection service on behalf of federal agencies
- Issuing written guidance for federal agencies on how to maintain efficient financial operations
- Reporting government-wide financial information for public and private use in the following publications: Daily and Monthly Treasury Statements, the Treasury Bulletin, and the Combined Statement of Receipts, Outlays and Balances of the U.S. Government

Federal agency appropriation

Recording appropriation and apportionment of the appropriation – Once Congress receives appropriated funds, a federal agency makes a journal entry, debiting Other Appropriations Realized and crediting Unapportioned Authority Available. To maintain accurate recordkeeping, other accounts may be created for appropriations that were granted for specific purposes. After a Treasury Warrant is issued, the Office of Management and Budget (OMB) then apportions the appropriation. The agency is now allowed to spend funds and incur obligations. It recognizes its apportionment during the first quarter by debiting Unapportioned Authority Available and crediting Apportionment. The Unapportioned Authority Available account serves as a record for how much of the appropriation has not yet been apportioned by the OMB but will be apportioned later. The OMB usually confers with agencies to determine an apportionment time period that is best suited to the agency's needs. As later apportionments are made, the Unapportioned Authority-Available account is reduced accordingly. It should be noted that reserve funds held for contingencies should be recorded separately from the apportionments of an appropriation.

<u>Allocating apportionments to their many programs</u> – In large federal agencies, there may be several programs requiring funding. To run the agency efficiently and to accurately disburse its apportioned appropriations, the agency identifies sub-components within it. It is to these sub-components that the agency will disburse allotted funds. Accounting records should reflect this method of allocation by debiting Apportionment and crediting Allotments. The allotment account then shows the amount of funds available to be used for the operations of the agency and its programs. At the end of the period, the allotment account expires and any balance of funds is forfeited. A negative balance should never occur, as spending beyond the allotment is prohibited.

Chief Financial Officers Act

In 1990, the Chief Financial Officers (CFO) Act was approved by Congress. The purpose of the act was to improve the accounting and financial management systems and their respective internal controls at the various agencies of the federal government. This in turn, would help ensure that the financial information released was reliable, allowing government programs to be more accurately evaluated. This was all to be done through statuary provisions. The act called for the appointment of Chief Financial Officers for each major executive agency. Also, the position of Deputy Director was created for the Office of Management and Budget. And finally, the act was also responsible for establishing the Office of Federal Financial Management. These changes were not only to improve financial management but also to stop financial mismanagement due to corruption.

Government Management Reform Act

As a means for ensuring the accuracy and reliability of government accounting, the Government Management Reform Act of 1994 requires the highest-ranking officials from the largest federal agencies in the executive branch to prepare an agency-wide audited financial statement. These financial statements, covering the most recently completed fiscal year, are to be submitted by March 1 to the Office of Management and Budgets (OMB). Also, under the Government Management Reform Act of 1994, the Secretary of Treasury is expected to prepare and submit the federal government's consolidated financial statements to the President and Congress by March 31. These consolidated financial statements are to be audited by the Comptroller General of the United States.

Federal Financial Management Improvement Act

The goals of the Federal Financial Management Improvement Act of 1996 include:
- Improving the federal government's cost controls by designing better financial management systems
- Raising accountability within federal financial management
- Strengthening the federal financial management's credibility

- Requiring federal financial data to fully disclose the total costs of its programs and activities
- Allowing for better comparisons between program costs to program results
- Increasing the federal financial management's overall efficiency and performance
- Ensuring federal agencies use consistent accounting practices from year to year
- Encouraging federal agencies to monitor their budgets

Making sure all executive branch federal agencies follow applicable accounting standards.

Commitment criteria

To ensure the availability of funds for a specific purchase, a journal entry must be made to reserve the budget authority. The entry would debit Commitments and credit Undelivered Orders in the amount needed for the purchase. While this is not legally binding, the entry serves as a budgeting tool for management.

For a commitment to be a binding agreement it must meet one or more of the following criteria:
- The agreement was entered into by relevant parties with the proper authority and executed before the appropriation's expiration.
- The goods, services, or other transactional items are described with adequate details.
- The loan agreement clearly states the terms of the loan and is valid.
- There is proof that the order placed with a federal agency was legally required.
- There is proof that the purchase was authorized without the use of advertising.
- There is pending litigation, which allows the apportionment to be obligated in the amount of the possible liability.

Available funds are obligated to cover any other legal liability.

Federal financial statement liabilities

Liabilities are measurable amounts of probable future cash flows. The federal financial statements show liabilities from the following types of transactions:
- *Exchange transactions that have already occurred:* These liabilities are recognized at the time of exchange; goods or services are received in exchange for an agreement to pay.
- *Non-exchange transactions:* These are liabilities to be paid in exchange for nothing. For example, the government pays social security benefits to citizens without receiving anything in exchange.

- 81 -

- *Government related events:* Liabilities resulting from an interaction between the federal government and its surrounding environment.
- *Government acknowledged events*: These liabilities are financial consequences from the government's acknowledgement of certain events.

Budgetary integrity

In the federal government and its agencies, budgetary integrity refers to the responsibilities the government has regarding the use of public funds and its obligations for reporting on those uses. Its responsibilities include monitoring the spending of public funds so that it stays within the legal appropriation limits. Also, the government or agency should ensure strict accountability for the way public funds are used. An obligation exists to provide useful and meaningful information in the financial and performance reports, as well as, to disclose the sources of budgetary resources in order to establish that the budgetary resources were acquired with legal authorization.

Stewardship objective

The federal government has the responsibility of managing the nation's financial operations and investments. The stewardship objective with regard to federal financial reporting is to ensure users receive a sufficient amount of information to assess the government's financial management; thus allowing users to determine if the government's financial decisions are benefiting the country currently and whether these decisions will add to the nation's future success. To fairly assess the government's financial position, both financial and non-financial information must be supplied. Examples of financial information include figures for assets and liabilities. Examples of non-financial information include figures for people on welfare, subsidized housing, and unemployment; these are often referred to as economic indicators. The stewardship of federal financial reporting requires the following information to be reported: the value of assets and liabilities, net amount, a debt analysis, unrecognized obligations, contingent liabilities, changes in debt service obligations, and changes in capital assets, as well as, their service potential.

It also requires the following supplemental information: the value of government investments in research and development; amount of activities with economic or social growth potential; future inflation rate estimates; projected current law budgets; contributions toward improving educational programs, preserving the environment, and assets that are not government owned; and finally consumer trends reflecting the national economy. All of this information, basic and supplemental, helps financial report users assess the nation's financial position and to determine if it has been improved, worsened, or simply maintained.

Past government financial reports

Federal financial reports provide information regarding the government's financial position during a specified time period. Reports of prior time periods are kept and used as reference tools. Analyzing and comparing the government's financial reports from prior periods to the current period allows users to recognize financial changes and evaluate their effects. Also officials responsible for budgetary planning use prior years' financial reports as a reference for determining whether current and future fiscal government years will be able to afford the same programs offered in the past. In budgetary resource planning, users look to the previous year's long-term financial obligations and consider their consequences. They also review the trust funds' financial positions and the backlog of deferred maintenance.

Funded and unfunded liabilities and Stewardship Assets

Funded liabilities are liabilities which may be covered by using, allocating, or spending budgetary resources. Unfunded liabilities are liabilities which may not be covered by budgetary resources unless permitted through an act by Congress. Federal agencies are required to disclose which liabilities are funded and which are unfunded in the Interior's financial statements.

According to GAAP, federal agencies are not required to report *Stewardship Assets* on the balance sheet nor disclose them in the notes. The reason for such leniency is due to the difficultness in determining relevant values for assets of this type.

Stewardship responsibilities

Stewardship responsibilities include the risks and responsibilities related to the government's finances and the federal insurance programs it offers, including the social insurance programs. While Stewardship responsibilities are not directly classified as traditional liabilities, they do report information to indicate whether the government's activities have improved or hurt its fiscal health. More specifically, reported stewardship responsibilities allow report users to determine if current programs will or will not be able to continue in the future, and whether there will be enough future budgetary resources to handle the anticipated future obligations.

Stewardship property, plant and equipment are physical assets similar in many respects to traditional property, plant and equipment; they differ, however, in that stewardship property, plant and equipment assets usually have indeterminate or irrelevant values, and so unlike traditional property, plant and equipment assets, they are not capitalized. Despite these differences, governments and their agencies are still required to report them and show accountability for them since they are assets. For reporting purposes, stewardship property, plant and equipment assets typically fall into one of two categories: land or heritage assets.

Stewardship investments

Stewardship investments are those investments that the federal government makes in human capital, research and development, and nonfederal physical property for the purpose of increasing the country's production so that the nation's economy improves or is at least maintained. Funds spent on stewardship investments are reported as expenses in the calculations of the net cost of operations. Stewardship investment reports must show an investment's expenses for the last five years, allowing report users to have a better understanding or expectation of future investment demands. These reports must also provide trend analyses of the investment's costs, outputs, and outcomes.

Management's Discussion and Analysis

The Federal Accounting Standards Advisory Board (FASAB) requires governments and their agencies to submit a Management's Discussion and Analysis as required supplementary information (RSI) to their financial reports. The Management's Discussion and Analysis conveys the manager's thoughts and opinions about the government or agency; it explains the entity's operations and helps clarify the general purpose financial statements. Within the Management's Discussion and analysis, FASAB requires the following items to be included: the general mission, the entity's organizational structure, performance goals and results, a financial statement analysis, the status of the agency's systems and controls, a record of its legal compliance, and resulting benefits of the agency's existence.

Performance and accountability report

The performance and accountability report (PAR) is used to determine and describe how an agency performs each year. This report takes into consideration the specific targets and goals that were assigned to the agency at the beginning of the fiscal year and measures the final results against them. These reports are used to keep the general public informed but also are used to determine whether the agency is making good use of their resources. This is another report that the House and Senate use when determining how to allocate funds in the next budget cycle.

Requirements for the US Consolidated Financial Report

The US Consolidated Financial Report is a bit like the State of the Union financial report in that it takes all of the financial data from the reports filed by federal agencies and departments and compiles them into one massive report that allows everyone to see the state of the United States government in one consolidated report. This report can then be analyzed to address federal management issues and overall fiscal challenges.

Components of the US Standard General Ledger

The US Standard General Ledger (USSGL) is a uniform chart of accounts and technical guidance that allows for the standardization of federal agency accounting. The ledger can be broken down into the following categories:
1. Chart of Accounts
2. Account Descriptions
3. Accounting Transactions
4. USSGL Attributes
5. Report Crosswalks
6. Reclassified Statements of Crosswalks
7. Government-Wide Treasury Account Symbol (GTAS) Validations and Edits

Required entries for recording the budget, modifying the budget, and recording expenditures

To record the budget, all revenue (debits) and expense recordings (credits) must be made to the appropriate ledger. This is an example.

General Ledger Acct	Acct Title	Debits	Credits
510	Estimated Revenues	30,000	
515	Estimated Other Financing Sources	100	
540	Appropriated Fund Balance	100	
900	Appropriations for Expenditures		30,000
905	Appropriations for Other Financing Uses		200

To modify the budget, the additional revenue and or expense must be recorded to the appropriate ledger. This is an example of the entries required for recording a modification to the budget.

General Ledger Acct	Acct Title	Debits	Credits
510	Estimated Revenue	500	
900	Appropriations		500

Practice Test

Practice Questions

1. Which statement most adequately describes interperiod equity?
    a. Previous year taxpayers have provided adequate resources to pay for the cost of current year services
    b. Previous year tax revenue is equal to budget amounts
    c. Current year costs are equal to the amount budgeted for the current year
    d. Current year taxpayers have provided adequate resources to pay for the cost of current year services

2. What is the purpose of the Governmental Accounting Standards Board?
    a. To establish standards of conduct for government accountants
    b. To establish and improve standards of accounting and financial reporting for U.S. state and local governments
    c. To indicate the differences between government accounting and private sector accounting
    d. To establish and improve standards of accounting and financial reporting for the U.S. federal government

3. "The Governmental Accounting Standards Board (GASB) uses due process when setting standards." Which best explains "due process" with respect to that statement?
    a. The GASB has a pre-determined process to develop concepts and standards
    b. The GASB carefully weighs the views of its constituents to develop concepts and standards
    c. The GASB identifies the scope issues to be addressed to develop concepts and standards
    d. The GASB uses a committee system to determine the viability of developing concepts and standards

4. Which inventory valuation method determines ending inventory based on the last goods that were purchased?
    a. First-in First-out
    b. Last-in First-out
    c. Average cost
    d. Specific identification

5. Under which basis of accounting are revenues recognized when goods are sold or services are performed?
    a. Cash basis
    b. Accrual basis
    c. Cost basis
    d. Modified accrual basis

6. Which of the following is not an objective of FASAB SFFAS 4: Managerial Cost Accounting Concepts and Standards?
    a. Providing program managers with relevant and reliable information relating costs to outputs and activities
    b. Providing relevant and reliable cost information to assist Congress and executives in making decisions
    c. Ensuring accuracy in accounting methods and reporting requirements of government agencies
    d. Ensuring consistency between costs reported in general purpose financial reports and costs reported to program managers

7. What is the purpose of variance analysis in managerial cost accounting?
    a. To measure the difference between actual revenues and forecasted revenues
    b. To determine why actual costs were different than budgeted costs
    c. To determine why actual revenues were different than forecasted revenues
    d. To measure the change in costs between two periods of time

8. Which approach to budgeting helps decision-makers determine the ability of a program to use inputs to affect a particular outcome?
    a. Zero based budgeting
    b. Line item budgeting
    c. Program budgeting
    d. Performance based budgeting

9. What is the proper sequence of the budget process?
    a. Policy planning, policy validation, policy execution, policy evaluation
    b. Policy planning, policy formulation, policy execution, policy evaluation
    c. Policy validation, policy execution, policy evaluation, policy implementation
    d. None of the above

10. Which type of budget is used to determine the most appropriate method for financing the purchase of equipment or the building of facilities?
    a. Facilities budget
    b. Capital cost budget
    c. Capital budget
    d. Investment resources budget

11. Which of the following is not a criterion when determining whether an organization is considered a component unit?
    a. The resources of the organization are for the benefit of the primary government
    b. The primary government is entitled to a majority of the economic resources of the organization
    c. The organization is fiscally responsible to the primary government
    d. The resources of the organization are significant to the primary government

12. Which item distinguishes the Comprehensive Annual Financial Report for the government from the Annual Financial Reports prepared by public sector companies?
    a. A statement of changes in financial position
    b. A statistical section
    c. A government executive summary
    d. Inclusion of financial ratios

13. Which accounting method is used by government funds?
    a. Cash accounting method
    b. Accrual accounting method
    c. Modified accrual accounting method
    d. Fund accounting method

14. Which government financial statement is similar to an income statement for a private sector organization?
    a. Statement of revenues and expenses
    b. Statement of activities
    c. Statement of cash disbursements
    d. Statement of revenue sharing

15. The Management's Discussion and Analysis section of government-wide financial statements provides information most suitable for a user to determine...
    a. whether the government's financial position has improved
    b. the types of services provided
    c. the fiscal responsibility of government managers
    d. the impact a service has on the community

16. Which item is included in the permanent fund of a government?
    a. Resources used for capital assets
    b. Funds to be used for a specified purpose
    c. Funds set aside to be invested to produce an income
    d. Everything not reported in another fund

17. Under which condition would an infrastructure asset not be required to be depreciated?
    a. When the government funds the infrastructure assets
    b. When the infrastructure asset is preserved at an established level
    c. When the infrastructure asset is financed through a special fund
    d. When there are adequate funds to maintain the infrastructure asset

18. A reserved fund balance signifies...
    a. the funds are intended to be used in a specified manner
    b. the funds are to be used to pay outstanding debt
    c. the funds are to be used for a specific purpose
    d. none of the above

19. Performing a reconciliation of the fund balance with Treasury accounts is important to...
    a. ensure the accuracy and timeliness of deposit and disbursement data
    b. report any differences between the reconciliation and the Treasury's General Ledger
    c. ensure that all checks and disbursements have cleared the Treasury
    d. determine the future economic benefits of monies spent by an agency

20. A reconciliation of the Standard General Ledger fund balance accounts is supported by...
    a. deposits in transit reconciliation
    b. undistributed reconciliation
    c. check issue reconciliation
    d. all of the above

21. Which is a consequence of failing to implement timely and effective reconciliation processes?
    a. Censure of the manager responsible for performing the reconciliation
    b. Decreases the balance of the fund account
    c. Increases the risk of fraud
    d. None of the above

22. Under the Government Performance Results Act of 1993, each government agency must develop a strategic plan for program activities that covers a period of at least how many years?
    a. Three
    b. Five
    c. Seven
    d. Ten

23. What does the Federal Credit Reform Act of 1990 govern?
   a. The credit limit of federal programs
   b. Budget authority of federal programs
   c. Federal programs that make direct loans
   d. Credit limits that federal programs may extend to local governments

24. What is the definition of a direct loan?
   a. A loan from the Treasury to a federal agency
   b. A loan from a federal agency to the Treasury
   c. A disbursement by the government to a non-federal borrower which must be repaid
   d. A loan from the government to the Treasury to cover agency budget deficits

25. How do Performance and Accountability Reports ensure the integrity of an agency's financial statements and the federal budget?
   a. Agency financial statements are audited by an independent auditor
   b. Agencies are accountable for agency performance
   c. They reduces the chance of inconsistencies between the financial statements and the budget
   d. Performance and Accountability Reports are prepared in accordance with Government Accounting Standards

Answer Key and Explanations

1. **D:** Current year taxpayers have provided adequate resources to pay for the cost of current year services. Interperiod equity is a concept wherein current taxpayers provide adequate funds to cover current benefits, leaving no burden to future taxpayers for current benefits. If interperiod equity exists, the government does not need to defer costs to the future, or use accumulated resources to pay for current period services, because current year revenues were sufficient to cover current year expenses. In financial reporting, interperiod equity is one of the criteria used to evaluate accountability and helps determine the future implications of a government's fiscal decisions. Interperiod equity is not perceived as a goal; the Government Accounting Standards Board, for instance, does not take a position on the concept's appropriateness

2. **B:** To establish and improve standards of accounting and financial reporting for U.S. state and local governments. The Governmental Accounting Standards Board (GASB) is an independent organization that establishes and improves standards of accounting and financial reporting for U.S. state and local governments. The GASB provides generally accepted accounting principles (GAAP) for use by state and local governments. Compliance with the GASB standards is enforced by state law and the audit process. By conforming with GASB standards, government officials maintain accountability and stewardship over public resources. The GASB also educates the public, financial statement preparers, and auditors regarding the information governments provide in financial statements.

3. **B:** The GASB carefully weighs the views of its constituents when developing concepts and standards. The Governmental Accounting Standards Board (GASB) begins due process when a project is considered for addition to the GASB's technical agenda. The process for adding a project to the agenda begins with research, identification of scope issues and issues to be addressed, and the preparation of a prospectus for discussion at a public meeting. Other due process documents may be prepared, depending on the alternatives or proposals to be reported. These may include a discussion memorandum, invitation to comment, preliminary views, and exposure draft.

4. **A:** First-in First-out. There are four types of inventory valuation methods:
   - First-in First-out uses the first goods that were purchased, or used, as the cost of production. These are the first goods to be sold and are considered the cost of sales. The ending inventory consists of those items that were purchased last and still remain in inventory
   - Last-in First-out uses the last goods that were purchased, or used, as the cost of production. These are the first goods to be sold and are considered the cost of sales. The ending inventory consists of those items that were purchased first and still remain in inventory

- Average cost calculates the average unit cost of goods by adding the beginning inventory to the purchases made during the period. The ending inventory amount is the average cost multiplied by the number of items remaining in inventory
- Specific identification bases inventory figures on the actual cost of those items remaining in inventory

5. B: Accrual basis. Accrual basis accounting recognizes revenues when goods are sold, or services are performed, regardless of when revenues are collected. Associated expenses are recognized in the same period the revenues are recognized
- Cash basis accounting recognizes revenues when revenues are received, regardless of when goods are sold or the services are performed. Expenses are recognized in the period in which the expenses are paid
- Modified accrual basis recognizes revenues when the revenues are received. Expenses are recognized when the expense is incurred, regardless of when the expenses are paid
- Cost basis is not an accounting method in the vein of accrual and cash bases, but instead a monetary value reflecting the original cost of an asset

6. C: Ensure accuracy in accounting methods and reporting requirements of government agencies. The goal of SFFAS 4: Managerial Cost Accounting Concepts and Standards is to provide reliable and timely information on the full cost of federal programs, and their activities and outputs. The Federal Accounting Standards Advisory Board (FASAB) set these standards so that the cost information can be used by Congress and federal executives in making decisions about allocating federal resources, authorizing and modifying programs, and evaluating program performance. The cost information can also be used by program managers in making managerial decisions to improve operating economy and efficiency.

7. B: To determine why actual costs were different than budgeted costs. Variance analysis is performed to obtain the difference between actual costs and the standard costs allowed in a budget for output. It evaluates financial performance and helps management understand present costs, in order to control future costs. The different cost components used in this calculation include volume variation, material cost variation, and labor cost variation. By separating the cost components, government financial managers can determine why actual costs were different from budgeted costs and take action to correct situations that caused the cost differences.

8. D: Performance-based budgeting. There are diverse approaches to budgeting. In each of them, outputs produced are related to outcomes, and used to measure how efficiently a government uses inputs to create outcomes. The approaches to budgeting include:
- Performance-based budgeting is used to determine the ability of a program to use inputs to affect a particular outcome

- Zero-based budgeting is a process where a budget is constructed based on the budget of the previous year
- Line item budgeting is a simple method of budgeting where inputs are determined based on the purpose of the program or system
- Program budgeting allocates resources based on the funding of a program

9. B: Policy planning, policy formulation, policy execution, policy evaluation. Governments create and approve budgets through a strict process. The four stages, in sequential order are:

1. Policy planning— the planning phase of the budget process, including resource analysis and revenue estimation
2. Policy formulation— financial managers determine budget amounts and decide how the budget is to be executed
3. Policy execution— budget is implemented and revisions are made to budget amounts, if needed
4. Policy evaluation — auditing the budget to determine reasons for any variances, and evaluating the budgeting process

10. C: Capital budget. A capital budget is also known as an investment appraisal. It's used in the planning process to determine whether investments in capital equipment and facilities (property, plant and equipment) are feasible. Capital investments may also include new products and services, and research and development projects. Many methods are used in the capital budgeting and decision making process including accounting rate of return, net present value, profitability index, internal rate of return, modified internal rate of return, and equivalent annuity.

11. C: The organization is fiscally responsible to the primary government. A component unit is an entity associated with a primary government, but not financially accountable to the primary government. While legally separate from the primary government, component units hold economic resources for the direct benefit of the primary government. To be considered a component unit, the following criteria must be met:

- The economic resources received or held by the separate entity are for the direct benefit of the primary government
- The primary government has access to a majority of the economic resources held by the separate entity
- The separate entity's economic resources, to which the primary government is entitled, are deemed significant to the primary government

12. B: A statistical section. A Comprehensive Annual Financial Report prepared by government entities has three major sections: Introductory, Financial and Statistical. Public sector Annual Financial Reports do not include the statistical section. In addition, the Comprehensive Annual Financial Report combines fund account financial information and Enterprise Authority accounting. The

Comprehensive Annual Financial Report contains the financial results of the reporting year along with the previous year's accumulations, and a section comparing period budget and actual financial results.

13. C: Modified accrual accounting method. Government funds use the modified accrual accounting method, in which revenue is recorded in the accounting records when it is collected and measurable, and expenses are recorded in the period in which the expense is incurred. There are two exceptions: (1) materials and supplies may be recorded either when purchased or when used, and (2) interest of long-term debt is recorded on the due date. Government funds include the general fund, special assessment fund, and capital projects fund, but do not include the enterprise fund, internal service fund, and trust and agency fund.

14. B: Statement of activities. Government financial statements report revenues and expenditures. They include a balance sheet, a reconciliation and a statement of activities, otherwise known as the income statement (or profit and loss) statement in the private sector. A cash flow statement may also be prepared to show the sources of revenue and the outflow of expenditures. The government financial statements prepared by federal government agencies must comply with the Chief Financial Officer Act and are regulated by the Office of Federal Financial Management. Government financial statements prepared by state and local governments follow the rules established by the Government Accounting Standards Board.

15. A: Whether the government's financial position has improved. The Management Discussion and Analysis (MD&A) section provides analysis by management of the entity's financial performance for a given year. This analysis is used to determine whether a government's financial position has improved or deteriorated based on the year's operating results. Government-wide financial statements measure current assets, current liabilities, long-term assets and long-term liabilities. Also included are all of the revenues and costs associated with providing services. The revenues and costs include collected revenues, accrued revenues, paid expenses and accrued expenses.

16. C: Funds set aside to be invested to produce an income. Governmental funds are accounts for the tax-supported activities of a government. A fund balance is the difference between the assets and liabilities in a governmental fund. The types of governmental funds include:
- The general fund, which includes an accounting of everything not reported in another fund
- Special revenue funds, which are used to report revenue sources used for a specific purpose
- Debt service funds, used to repay debt

- Capital project funds, which track the accumulation and use of resources for constructing, acquiring and rehabilitating capital assets
- Permanent funds, containing principal amounts invested to produce income

17. B: When the infrastructure asset is preserved at an established level. Infrastructure assets are long-term capital assets that are stationary and have a longer life expectancy than most capital assets. They include roads, bridges, water systems, dams and lighting systems. Infrastructure assets do not need to be depreciated under the following conditions:
- The infrastructure asset is managed using an asset management system that has an up to date inventory, condition level assessments are performed and summarized using a measurement scale, and the maintenance costs are estimated and disclosed
- The infrastructure asset is preserved at, or above, an established level, with this condition level disclosed

18. C: The funds are to be used for a specific purpose. The fund balance is the amount that remains after the government Fund's assets have been used to pay the liabilities. Fund balance is reported as either reserved or unreserved.
- A reserved fund balance signifies that the fund's resources cannot be appropriated and spent, or that the resources are reserved for a particular purpose
- An unreserved fund balance signifies that the fund's resources can be used for any purpose as long as it is applied to that fund and the purpose of the fund

19. A: Ensure the accuracy and timeliness of deposit and disbursement data. Financial managers reconcile their agency's fund balance with Treasury accounts to assure accuracy and timeliness of deposit and disbursement data is reflected in the Fund Balance with Treasury Accounts. Each agency has internal control systems in place to ensure that all funds are correctly recorded and accounted. When there are errors in the reconciliation, the manager should determine the conditions that created the differences.

20. D: All of the above. The U.S. Treasury has designed three major central reconciliation processes to support the reconciliation of Standard General Ledger fund balance accounts, and the internal verification of ledgers that have supporting documentation. These reconciliation processes compare monthly cash receipt and disbursement transactions reported by federal agencies to data reported by other entities. These reconciliations ensure the accuracy and financial integrity of the Government's receipts and disbursements. They include:
- Deposits-in-transit reconciliation (SOD for Deposits)
- Undistributed reconciliation (SOD for Disbursements)
- Check issue reconciliation

21. C: Increases the risk of fraud. The consequences of failing to implement timely and effective reconciliation processes include:
- Increase in the risk of fraud, waste and mismanagement of funds
- Decrease of government's ability to effectively monitor budget execution
- Decrease of government's ability to accurately measure the full cost of government programs

Agencies should be reconciling Funds Balance with Treasury accounts monthly, officials should review and sign the monthly agency reconciliation documents, and make them available to auditors of agency financial statements and the U.S. Treasury's Financial Management Service upon request. Additionally, agencies should have written standard operating procedures to direct and document the correct reconciliation process.

22. B: Five. The head of each federal agency is required to submit a strategic plan for program activities to the Director of the Office of Management and Budget, and to Congress. This plan is to cover a period of no less than five years, and be updated at least every three years. The plan includes:
- A mission statement of the major functions and operations of the agency
- The general goals, objectives, and outcome for the functions and operations of the agency
- A description of how the goals and objectives are to be achieved
- A description of how the performance goals are related to the general goals and objectives
- Identification of key factors beyond the agency's control that may affect the achievement of the general goals and objectives
- A description of the program evaluations used in establishing or revising general goals and objectives

23. C: Federal programs that make direct loans. The Federal Credit Reform Act of 1990 governs federal credit programs that make direct loans and loan guarantees. The Act prescribes a special budget treatment for direct loans and loan guarantees that measures subsidy cost, rather than cash flows. For most credit programs, Congress must provide budget authority equal to the subsidy cost in annual appropriations acts before the program can make direct loans or loan guarantees.

24. C: A disbursement by the government to a non-federal borrower which must be repaid. A direct loan is a disbursement of funds by the U.S. Government to a non-federal borrower. The disbursement is made under a contract that requires repayment, either with or without interest. A direct loan may be made for the purchase of, or participation in, a loan made by another lender. Financing arrangements for this loan defer payment for more than 90 days, including the sale of a government asset on credit terms. A direct loan does not include the acquisition of a federally-guaranteed loan in satisfaction of default claims or the price support loans of the Commodity Credit Corporation.

25. C: They reduce the chance of inconsistencies between the financial statements and the budget. Linkage between budgetary information presented in the financial statements and the federal budget ensures the integrity of the numbers presented. To avoid inconsistencies:

- Agencies should ensure that the budgetary information used to prepare the Statement of Budgetary Resources (SBR) is consistent with the budgetary information reported to the Federal Agencies' Centralized Trial Balance System.
- Agencies should post subsequent changes to the budget preparation system of the executive branch's Office of Management and Budget
- Agencies should discuss any material changes to budgetary information subsequent to the publication of the audited Statement of Budgetary Resources (SBR) with their auditors to determine if restatement or note disclosure is necessary

Secret Key #1 - Time is Your Greatest Enemy

Pace Yourself

Wear a watch. At the beginning of the test, check the time (or start a chronometer on your watch to count the minutes), and check the time after every few questions to make sure you are "on schedule."

If you are forced to speed up, do it efficiently. Usually one or more answer choices can be eliminated without too much difficulty. Above all, don't panic. Don't speed up and just begin guessing at random choices. By pacing yourself, and continually monitoring your progress against your watch, you will always know exactly how far ahead or behind you are with your available time. If you find that you are one minute behind on the test, don't skip one question without spending any time on it, just to catch back up. Take 15 fewer seconds on the next four questions, and after four questions you'll have caught back up. Once you catch back up, you can continue working each problem at your normal pace.

Furthermore, don't dwell on the problems that you were rushed on. If a problem was taking up too much time and you made a hurried guess, it must be difficult. The difficult questions are the ones you are most likely to miss anyway, so it isn't a big loss. It is better to end with more time than you need than to run out of time.

Lastly, sometimes it is beneficial to slow down if you are constantly getting ahead of time. You are always more likely to catch a careless mistake by working more slowly than quickly, and among very high-scoring test takers (those who are likely to have lots of time left over), careless errors affect the score more than mastery of material.

Secret Key #2 - Guessing is not Guesswork

You probably know that guessing is a good idea. Unlike other standardized tests, there is no penalty for getting a wrong answer. Even if you have no idea about a question, you still have a 20-25% chance of getting it right.

Most test takers do not understand the impact that proper guessing can have on their score. Unless you score extremely high, guessing will significantly contribute to your final score.

Monkeys Take the Test

What most test takers don't realize is that to insure that 20-25% chance, you have to guess randomly. If you put 20 monkeys in a room to take this test, assuming they answered once per question and behaved themselves, on average they would get 20-25% of the questions correct. Put 20 test takers in the room, and the average will be much lower among guessed questions. Why?
1. The test writers intentionally write deceptive answer choices that "look" right. A test taker has no idea about a question, so he picks the "best looking" answer, which is often wrong. The monkey has no idea what looks good and what doesn't, so it will consistently be right about 20-25% of the time.
2. Test takers will eliminate answer choices from the guessing pool based on a hunch or intuition. Simple but correct answers often get excluded, leaving a 0% chance of being correct. The monkey has no clue, and often gets lucky with the best choice.

This is why the process of elimination endorsed by most test courses is flawed and detrimental to your performance. Test takers don't guess; they make an ignorant stab in the dark that is usually worse than random.

$5 Challenge

Let me introduce one of the most valuable ideas of this course—the $5 challenge:

You only mark your "best guess" if you are willing to bet $5 on it.
You only eliminate choices from guessing if you are willing to bet $5 on it.

Why $5? Five dollars is an amount of money that is small yet not insignificant, and can really add up fast (20 questions could cost you $100). Likewise, each answer choice on one question of the test will have a small impact on your overall score, but it can really add up to a lot of points in the end.

The process of elimination IS valuable. The following shows your chance of guessing it right:

If you eliminate wrong answer choices until only this many remain:	Chance of getting it correct:
1	100%
2	50%
3	33%

However, if you accidentally eliminate the right answer or go on a hunch for an incorrect answer, your chances drop dramatically—to 0%. By guessing among all the answer choices, you are GUARANTEED to have a shot at the right answer.

That's why the $5 test is so valuable. If you give up the advantage and safety of a pure guess, it had better be worth the risk.

What we still haven't covered is how to be sure that whatever guess you make is truly random. Here's the easiest way:

Always pick the first answer choice among those remaining.

Such a technique means that you have decided, **before you see a single test question**, exactly how you are going to guess, and since the order of choices tells you nothing about which one is correct, this guessing technique is perfectly random.

This section is not meant to scare you away from making educated guesses or eliminating choices; you just need to define when a choice is worth eliminating. The $5 test, along with a pre-defined random guessing strategy, is the best way to make sure you reap all of the benefits of guessing.

Secret Key #3 - Practice Smarter, Not Harder

Many test takers delay the test preparation process because they dread the awful amounts of practice time they think necessary to succeed on the test. We have refined an effective method that will take you only a fraction of the time.

There are a number of "obstacles" in the path to success. Among these are answering questions, finishing in time, and mastering test-taking strategies. All must be executed on the day of the test at peak performance, or your score will suffer. The test is a mental marathon that has a large impact on your future.

Just like a marathon runner, it is important to work your way up to the full challenge. So first you just worry about questions, and then time, and finally strategy:

Success Strategy

1. Find a good source for practice tests.
2. If you are willing to make a larger time investment, consider using more than one study guide. Often the different approaches of multiple authors will help you "get" difficult concepts.
3. Take a practice test with no time constraints, with all study helps, "open book." Take your time with questions and focus on applying strategies.
4. Take a practice test with time constraints, with all guides, "open book."
5. Take a final practice test without open material and with time limits.

If you have time to take more practice tests, just repeat step 5. By gradually exposing yourself to the full rigors of the test environment, you will condition your mind to the stress of test day and maximize your success.

Secret Key #4 - Prepare, Don't Procrastinate

Let me state an obvious fact: if you take the test three times, you will probably get three different scores. This is due to the way you feel on test day, the level of preparedness you have, and the version of the test you see. Despite the test writers' claims to the contrary, some versions of the test WILL be easier for you than others.

Since your future depends so much on your score, you should maximize your chances of success. In order to maximize the likelihood of success, you've got to prepare in advance. This means taking practice tests and spending time learning the information and test taking strategies you will need to succeed.

Never go take the actual test as a "practice" test, expecting that you can just take it again if you need to. Take all the practice tests you can on your own, but when you go to take the official test, be prepared, be focused, and do your best the first time!

Secret Key #5 - Test Yourself

Everyone knows that time is money. There is no need to spend too much of your time or too little of your time preparing for the test. You should only spend as much of your precious time preparing as is necessary for you to get the score you need.

Once you have taken a practice test under real conditions of time constraints, then you will know if you are ready for the test or not.

If you have scored extremely high the first time that you take the practice test, then there is not much point in spending countless hours studying. You are already there.

Benchmark your abilities by retaking practice tests and seeing how much you have improved. Once you consistently score high enough to guarantee success, then you are ready.

If you have scored well below where you need, then knuckle down and begin studying in earnest. Check your improvement regularly through the use of practice tests under real conditions. Above all, don't worry, panic, or give up. The key is perseverance!

Then, when you go to take the test, remain confident and remember how well you did on the practice tests. If you can score high enough on a practice test, then you can do the same on the real thing.

General Strategies

The most important thing you can do is to ignore your fears and jump into the test immediately. Do not be overwhelmed by any strange-sounding terms. You have to jump into the test like jumping into a pool—all at once is the easiest way.

Make Predictions

As you read and understand the question, try to guess what the answer will be. Remember that several of the answer choices are wrong, and once you begin reading them, your mind will immediately become cluttered with answer choices designed to throw you off. Your mind is typically the most focused immediately after you have read the question and digested its contents. If you can, try to predict what the correct answer will be. You may be surprised at what you can predict.

Quickly scan the choices and see if your prediction is in the listed answer choices. If it is, then you can be quite confident that you have the right answer. It still won't hurt to check the other answer choices, but most of the time, you've got it!

Answer the Question

It may seem obvious to only pick answer choices that answer the question, but the test writers can create some excellent answer choices that are wrong. Don't pick an answer just because it sounds right, or you believe it to be true. It MUST answer the question. Once you've made your selection, always go back and check it against the question and make sure that you didn't misread the question and that the answer choice does answer the question posed.

Benchmark

After you read the first answer choice, decide if you think it sounds correct or not. If it doesn't, move on to the next answer choice. If it does, mentally mark that answer choice. This doesn't mean that you've definitely selected it as your answer choice, it just means that it's the best you've seen thus far. Go ahead and read the next choice. If the next choice is worse than the one you've already selected, keep going to the next answer choice. If the next choice is better than the choice you've already selected, mentally mark the new answer choice as your best guess.

The first answer choice that you select becomes your standard. Every other answer choice must be benchmarked against that standard. That choice is correct until proven otherwise by another answer choice beating it out. Once you've decided that no other answer choice seems as good, do one final check to ensure that your answer choice answers the question posed.

Valid Information

Don't discount any of the information provided in the question. Every piece of information may be necessary to determine the correct answer. None of the information in the question is there to throw you off (while the answer choices will certainly have information to throw you off). If two seemingly unrelated topics are discussed, don't ignore either. You can be confident there is a relationship, or it wouldn't be included in the question, and you are probably going to have to determine what is that relationship to find the answer.

Avoid "Fact Traps"

Don't get distracted by a choice that is factually true. Your search is for the answer that answers the question. Stay focused and don't fall for an answer that is true but irrelevant. Always go back to the question and make sure you're choosing an answer that actually answers the question and is not just a true statement. An answer can be factually correct, but it MUST answer the question asked. Additionally, two answers can both be seemingly correct, so be sure to read all of the answer choices, and make sure that you get the one that BEST answers the question.

Milk the Question

Some of the questions may throw you completely off. They might deal with a subject you have not been exposed to, or one that you haven't reviewed in years. While your lack of knowledge about the subject will be a hindrance, the question itself can give you many clues that will help you find the correct answer. Read the question carefully and look for clues. Watch particularly for adjectives and nouns describing difficult terms or words that you don't recognize. Regardless of whether you completely understand a word or not, replacing it with a synonym, either provided or one you more familiar with, may help you to understand what the questions are asking. Rather than wracking your mind about specific detailed information concerning a difficult term or word, try to use mental substitutes that are easier to understand.

The Trap of Familiarity

Don't just choose a word because you recognize it. On difficult questions, you may not recognize a number of words in the answer choices. The test writers don't put "make-believe" words on the test, so don't think that just because you only recognize all the words in one answer choice that that answer choice must be correct. If you only recognize words in one answer choice, then focus on that one. Is it correct? Try your best to determine if it is correct. If it is, that's great. If not, eliminate it. Each word and answer choice you eliminate increases your chances of getting the question correct, even if you then have to guess among the unfamiliar choices.

Eliminate Answers

Eliminate choices as soon as you realize they are wrong. But be careful! Make sure you consider all of the possible answer choices. Just because one appears right, doesn't mean that the next one won't be even better! The test writers will usually put more than one good answer choice for every question, so read all of them. Don't worry if you are stuck between two that seem right. By getting down to just two remaining possible choices, your odds are now 50/50. Rather than wasting too much time, play the odds. You are guessing, but guessing wisely because you've been able to knock out some of the answer choices that you know are wrong. If you are eliminating choices and realize that the last answer choice you are left with is also obviously wrong, don't panic. Start over and consider each choice again. There may easily be something that you missed the first time and will realize on the second pass.

Tough Questions

If you are stumped on a problem or it appears too hard or too difficult, don't waste time. Move on! Remember though, if you can quickly check for obviously incorrect answer choices, your chances of guessing correctly are greatly improved. Before you completely give up, at least try to knock out a couple of possible answers. Eliminate what you can and then guess at the remaining answer choices before moving on.

Brainstorm

If you get stuck on a difficult question, spend a few seconds quickly brainstorming. Run through the complete list of possible answer choices. Look at each choice and ask yourself, "Could this answer the question satisfactorily?" Go through each answer choice and consider it independently of the others. By systematically going through all possibilities, you may find something that you would otherwise overlook. Remember though that when you get stuck, it's important to try to keep moving.

Read Carefully

Understand the problem. Read the question and answer choices carefully. Don't miss the question because you misread the terms. You have plenty of time to read each question thoroughly and make sure you understand what is being asked. Yet a happy medium must be attained, so don't waste too much time. You must read carefully, but efficiently.

Face Value

When in doubt, use common sense. Always accept the situation in the problem at face value. Don't read too much into it. These problems will not require you to make huge leaps of logic. The test writers aren't trying to throw you off with a cheap trick. If you have to go beyond creativity and make a leap of logic in order to have an answer choice answer the question, then you should look at the other answer choices. Don't overcomplicate the problem by creating theoretical relationships or explanations that will warp time or space. These are normal problems rooted in reality. It's just that the applicable relationship or explanation may not be readily apparent and you have to figure things out. Use your common sense to interpret anything that isn't clear.

Prefixes

If you're having trouble with a word in the question or answer choices, try dissecting it. Take advantage of every clue that the word might include. Prefixes and suffixes can be a huge help. Usually they allow you to determine a basic meaning. Pre- means before, post- means after, pro - is positive, de- is negative. From these prefixes and suffixes, you can get an idea of the general meaning of the word and try to put it into context. Beware though of any traps. Just because con- is the opposite of pro-, doesn't necessarily mean congress is the opposite of progress!

Hedge Phrases

Watch out for critical hedge phrases, led off with words such as "likely," "may," "can," "sometimes," "often," "almost," "mostly," "usually," "generally," "rarely," and "sometimes." Question writers insert these hedge phrases to cover every possibility. Often an answer choice will be wrong simply because it leaves no room for exception. Unless the situation calls for them, avoid answer choices that have definitive words like "exactly," and "always."

Switchback Words

Stay alert for "switchbacks." These are the words and phrases frequently used to alert you to shifts in thought. The most common switchback word is "but." Others include "although," "however," "nevertheless," "on the other hand," "even though," "while," "in spite of," "despite," and "regardless of."

New Information

Correct answer choices will rarely have completely new information included. Answer choices typically are straightforward reflections of the material asked about and will directly relate to the question. If a new piece of information is included in an answer choice that doesn't even seem to relate to the topic being asked about, then that answer choice is likely incorrect. All of the information needed to answer the question is usually provided for you in the question. You should not have to make guesses that are unsupported or choose answer choices that require unknown information that cannot be reasoned from what is given.

Time Management

On technical questions, don't get lost on the technical terms. Don't spend too much time on any one question. If you don't know what a term means, then odds are you aren't going to get much further since you don't have a dictionary. You should be able to immediately recognize whether or not you know a term. If you don't, work with the other clues that you have—the other answer choices and terms provided— but don't waste too much time trying to figure out a difficult term that you don't know.

Contextual Clues

Look for contextual clues. An answer can be right but not the correct answer. The contextual clues will help you find the answer that is most right and is correct. Understand the context in which a phrase or statement is made. This will help you make important distinctions.

Don't Panic

Panicking will not answer any questions for you; therefore, it isn't helpful. When you first see the question, if your mind goes blank, take a deep breath. Force yourself to mechanically go through the steps of solving the problem using the strategies you've learned.

Pace Yourself

Don't get clock fever. It's easy to be overwhelmed when you're looking at a page full of questions, your mind is full of random thoughts and feeling confused, and the clock is ticking down faster than you would like. Calm down and maintain the pace that you have set for yourself. As long as you are on track by monitoring your pace, you are guaranteed to have enough time for yourself. When you get to the last few minutes of the test, it may seem like you won't have enough time left, but if you only have as many questions as you should have left at that point, then you're right on track!

Answer Selection

The best way to pick an answer choice is to eliminate all of those that are wrong, until only one is left and confirm that is the correct answer. Sometimes though, an answer choice may immediately look right. Be careful! Take a second to make sure that the other choices are not equally obvious. Don't make a hasty mistake. There are only two times that you should stop before checking other answers. First is when you are positive that the answer choice you have selected is correct. Second is when time is almost out and you have to make a quick guess!

Check Your Work

Since you will probably not know every term listed and the answer to every question, it is important that you get credit for the ones that you do know. Don't miss any questions through careless mistakes. If at all possible, try to take a second to look back over your answer selection and make sure you've selected the correct answer choice and haven't made a costly careless mistake (such as marking an answer choice that you didn't mean to mark). The time it takes for this quick double check should more than pay for itself in caught mistakes.

Beware of Directly Quoted Answers

Sometimes an answer choice will repeat word for word a portion of the question or reference section. However, beware of such exact duplication. It may be a trap! More than likely, the correct choice will paraphrase or summarize a point, rather than being exactly the same wording.

Slang

Scientific sounding answers are better than slang ones. An answer choice that begins "To compare the outcomes..." is much more likely to be correct than one that begins "Because some people insisted..."

Extreme Statements

Avoid wild answers that throw out highly controversial ideas that are proclaimed as established fact. An answer choice that states the "process should used in certain situations, if..." is much more likely to be correct than one that states the "process should be discontinued completely." The first is a calm rational statement and doesn't even make a definitive, uncompromising stance, using a hedge word "if" to provide wiggle room, whereas the second choice is a radical idea and far more extreme.

Answer Choice Families

When you have two or more answer choices that are direct opposites or parallels, one of them is usually the correct answer. For instance, if one answer choice states "x increases" and another answer choice states "x decreases" or "y increases," then those two or three answer choices are very similar in construction and fall into the same family of answer choices. A family of answer choices consists of two or three answer choices, very similar in construction, but often with directly opposite meanings. Usually the correct answer choice will be in that family of answer choices. The "odd man out" or answer choice that doesn't seem to fit the parallel construction of the other answer choices is more likely to be incorrect.

Special Report: How to Overcome Test Anxiety

The very nature of tests caters to some level of anxiety, nervousness, or tension, just as we feel for any important event that occurs in our lives. A little bit of anxiety or nervousness can be a good thing. It helps us with motivation, and makes achievement just that much sweeter. However, too much anxiety can be a problem, especially if it hinders our ability to function and perform.

"Test anxiety," is the term that refers to the emotional reactions that some test-takers experience when faced with a test or exam. Having a fear of testing and exams is based upon a rational fear, since the test-taker's performance can shape the course of an academic career. Nevertheless, experiencing excessive fear of examinations will only interfere with the test-taker's ability to perform and chance to be successful.

There are a large variety of causes that can contribute to the development and sensation of test anxiety. These include, but are not limited to, lack of preparation and worrying about issues surrounding the test.

Lack of Preparation

Lack of preparation can be identified by the following behaviors or situations:

Not scheduling enough time to study, and therefore cramming the night before the test or exam
Managing time poorly, to create the sensation that there is not enough time to do everything
Failing to organize the text information in advance, so that the study material consists of the entire text and not simply the pertinent information
Poor overall studying habits

Worrying, on the other hand, can be related to both the test taker, or many other factors around him/her that will be affected by the results of the test. These include worrying about:

Previous performances on similar exams, or exams in general
How friends and other students are achieving
The negative consequences that will result from a poor grade or failure

There are three primary elements to test anxiety. Physical components, which involve the same typical bodily reactions as those to acute anxiety (to be discussed below). Emotional factors have to do with fear or panic. Mental or cognitive issues concerning attention spans and memory abilities.

Physical Signals

There are many different symptoms of test anxiety, and these are not limited to mental and emotional strain. Frequently there are a range of physical signals that will let a test taker know that he/she is suffering from test anxiety. These bodily changes can include the following:

Perspiring
Sweaty palms
Wet, trembling hands
Nausea
Dry mouth
A knot in the stomach
Headache
Faintness
Muscle tension
Aching shoulders, back and neck
Rapid heart beat
Feeling too hot/cold

To recognize the sensation of test anxiety, a test-taker should monitor him/herself for the following sensations:

The physical distress symptoms as listed above
Emotional sensitivity, expressing emotional feelings such as the need to cry or laugh too much, or a sensation of anger or helplessness
A decreased ability to think, causing the test-taker to blank out or have racing thoughts that are hard to organize or control.

Though most students will feel some level of anxiety when faced with a test or exam, the majority can cope with that anxiety and maintain it at a manageable level. However, those who cannot are faced with a very real and very serious condition, which can and should be controlled for the immeasurable benefit of this sufferer.

Naturally, these sensations lead to negative results for the testing experience. The most common effects of test anxiety have to do with nervousness and mental blocking.

Nervousness

Nervousness can appear in several different levels:

The test-taker's difficulty, or even inability to read and understand the questions on the test

The difficulty or inability to organize thoughts to a coherent form

The difficulty or inability to recall key words and concepts relating to the testing questions (especially essays)

The receipt of poor grades on a test, though the test material was well known by the test taker

Conversely, a person may also experience mental blocking, which involves:

Blanking out on test questions

Only remembering the correct answers to the questions when the test has already finished.

Fortunately for test anxiety sufferers, beating these feelings, to a large degree, has to do with proper preparation. When a test taker has a feeling of preparedness, then anxiety will be dramatically lessened.

The first step to resolving anxiety issues is to distinguish which of the two types of anxiety are being suffered. If the anxiety is a direct result of a lack of preparation, this should be considered a normal reaction, and the anxiety level (as opposed to the test results) shouldn't be anything to worry about. However, if, when adequately prepared, the test-taker still panics, blanks out, or seems to overreact, this is not a fully rational reaction. While this can be considered normal too, there are many ways to combat and overcome these effects.

Remember that anxiety cannot be entirely eliminated, however, there are ways to minimize it, to make the anxiety easier to manage. Preparation is one of the best ways to minimize test anxiety. Therefore the following techniques are wise in order to best fight off any anxiety that may want to build.

To begin with, try to avoid cramming before a test, whenever it is possible. By trying to memorize an entire term's worth of information in one day, you'll be shocking your system, and not giving yourself a very good chance to absorb the information. This is an easy path to anxiety, so for those who suffer from test anxiety, cramming should not even be considered an option.

Instead of cramming, work throughout the semester to combine all of the material which is presented throughout the semester, and work on it gradually as the course goes by, making sure to master the main concepts first, leaving minor details for a week or so before the test.

To study for the upcoming exam, be sure to pose questions that may be on the examination, to gauge the ability to answer them by integrating the ideas from your texts, notes and lectures, as well as any supplementary readings.

If it is truly impossible to cover all of the information that was covered in that particular term, concentrate on the most important portions, that can be covered very well. Learn these concepts as best as possible, so that when the test comes, a goal can be made to use these concepts as presentations of your knowledge.

In addition to study habits, changes in attitude are critical to beating a struggle with test anxiety. In fact, an improvement of the perspective over the entire test-taking experience can actually help a test taker to enjoy studying and therefore improve the overall experience. Be certain not to overemphasize the significance of the grade - know that the result of the test is neither a reflection of self worth, nor is it a measure of intelligence; one grade will not predict a person's future success.

To improve an overall testing outlook, the following steps should be tried:

Keeping in mind that the most reasonable expectation for taking a test is to expect to try to demonstrate as much of what you know as you possibly can. Reminding ourselves that a test is only one test; this is not the only one, and there will be others.
The thought of thinking of oneself in an irrational, all-or-nothing term should be avoided at all costs.
A reward should be designated for after the test, so there's something to look forward to. Whether it be going to a movie, going out to eat, or simply visiting friends, schedule it in advance, and do it no matter what result is expected on the exam.

Test-takers should also keep in mind that the basics are some of the most important things, even beyond anti-anxiety techniques and studying. Never neglect the basic social, emotional and biological needs, in order to try to absorb information. In order to best achieve, these three factors must be held as just as important as the studying itself.

Study Steps

Remember the following important steps for studying:

Maintain healthy nutrition and exercise habits. Continue both your recreational activities and social pass times. These both contribute to your physical and emotional well being.
Be certain to get a good amount of sleep, especially the night before the test, because when you're overtired you are not able to perform to the best of your best ability.
Keep the studying pace to a moderate level by taking breaks when they are needed, and varying the work whenever possible, to keep the mind fresh instead of getting bored.
When enough studying has been done that all the material that can be learned has been learned, and the test taker is prepared for the test, stop studying and do

something relaxing such as listening to music, watching a movie, or taking a warm bubble bath.

There are also many other techniques to minimize the uneasiness or apprehension that is experienced along with test anxiety before, during, or even after the examination. In fact, there are a great deal of things that can be done to stop anxiety from interfering with lifestyle and performance. Again, remember that anxiety will not be eliminated entirely, and it shouldn't be. Otherwise that "up" feeling for exams would not exist, and most of us depend on that sensation to perform better than usual. However, this anxiety has to be at a level that is manageable.

Of course, as we have just discussed, being prepared for the exam is half the battle right away. Attending all classes, finding out what knowledge will be expected on the exam, and knowing the exam schedules are easy steps to lowering anxiety. Keeping up with work will remove the need to cram, and efficient study habits will eliminate wasted time. Studying should be done in an ideal location for concentration, so that it is simple to become interested in the material and give it complete attention. A method such as SQ3R (Survey, Question, Read, Recite, Review) is a wonderful key to follow to make sure that the study habits are as effective as possible, especially in the case of learning from a textbook. Flashcards are great techniques for memorization. Learning to take good notes will mean that notes will be full of useful information, so that less sifting will need to be done to seek out what is pertinent for studying. Reviewing notes after class and then again on occasion will keep the information fresh in the mind. From notes that have been taken summary sheets and outlines can be made for simpler reviewing.

A study group can also be a very motivational and helpful place to study, as there will be a sharing of ideas, all of the minds can work together, to make sure that everyone understands, and the studying will be made more interesting because it will be a social occasion.

Basically, though, as long as the test-taker remains organized and self confident, with efficient study habits, less time will need to be spent studying, and higher grades will be achieved.

To become self confident, there are many useful steps. The first of these is "self talk." It has been shown through extensive research, that self-talk for students who suffer from test anxiety, should be well monitored, in order to make sure that it contributes to self confidence as opposed to sinking the student. Frequently the self talk of test-anxious students is negative or self-defeating, thinking that everyone else is smarter and faster, that they always mess up, and that if they don't do well, they'll fail the entire course. It is important to decreasing anxiety that awareness is made of self talk. Try writing any negative self thoughts and then disputing them with a positive statement instead. Begin self-encouragement as though it was a friend speaking. Repeat positive statements to help reprogram the mind to believing in successes instead of failures.

Helpful Techniques

Other extremely helpful techniques include:

Self-visualization of doing well and reaching goals
While aiming for an "A" level of understanding, don't try to "overprotect" by setting your expectations lower. This will only convince the mind to stop studying in order to meet the lower expectations.
Don't make comparisons with the results or habits of other students. These are individual factors, and different things work for different people, causing different results.
Strive to become an expert in learning what works well, and what can be done in order to improve. Consider collecting this data in a journal.
Create rewards for after studying instead of doing things before studying that will only turn into avoidance behaviors.
Make a practice of relaxing - by using methods such as progressive relaxation, self-hypnosis, guided imagery, etc - in order to make relaxation an automatic sensation.
Work on creating a state of relaxed concentration so that concentrating will take on the focus of the mind, so that none will be wasted on worrying.
Take good care of the physical self by eating well and getting enough sleep.
Plan in time for exercise and stick to this plan.

Beyond these techniques, there are other methods to be used before, during and after the test that will help the test-taker perform well in addition to overcoming anxiety.

Before the exam comes the academic preparation. This involves establishing a study schedule and beginning at least one week before the actual date of the test. By doing this, the anxiety of not having enough time to study for the test will be automatically eliminated. Moreover, this will make the studying a much more effective experience, ensuring that the learning will be an easier process. This relieves much undue pressure on the test-taker.

Summary sheets, note cards, and flash cards with the main concepts and examples of these main concepts should be prepared in advance of the actual studying time. A topic should never be eliminated from this process. By omitting a topic because it isn't expected to be on the test is only setting up the test-taker for anxiety should it actually appear on the exam. Utilize the course syllabus for laying out the topics that should be studied. Carefully go over the notes that were made in class, paying special attention to any of the issues that the professor took special care to emphasize while lecturing in class. In the textbooks, use the chapter review, or if possible, the chapter tests, to begin your review.

It may even be possible to ask the instructor what information will be covered on the exam, or what the format of the exam will be (for example, multiple choice, essay, free form, true-false). Additionally, see if it is possible to find out how many questions will be on the test. If a review sheet or sample test has been offered by the professor, make good use of it, above anything else, for the preparation for the test. Another great resource for getting to know the examination is reviewing tests from previous semesters. Use these tests to review, and aim to achieve a 100% score on each of the possible topics. With a few exceptions, the goal that you set for yourself is the highest one that you will reach.

Take all of the questions that were assigned as homework, and rework them to any other possible course material. The more problems reworked, the more skill and confidence will form as a result. When forming the solution to a problem, write out each of the steps. Don't simply do head work. By doing as many steps on paper as possible, much clarification and therefore confidence will be formed. Do this with as many homework problems as possible, before checking the answers. By checking the answer after each problem, a reinforcement will exist, that will not be on the exam. Study situations should be as exam-like as possible, to prime the test-taker's system for the experience. By waiting to check the answers at the end, a psychological advantage will be formed, to decrease the stress factor.

Another fantastic reason for not cramming is the avoidance of confusion in concepts, especially when it comes to mathematics. 8-10 hours of study will become one hundred percent more effective if it is spread out over a week or at least several days, instead of doing it all in one sitting. Recognize that the human brain requires time in order to assimilate new material, so frequent breaks and a span of study time over several days will be much more beneficial.

Additionally, don't study right up until the point of the exam. Studying should stop a minimum of one hour before the exam begins. This allows the brain to rest and put things in their proper order. This will also provide the time to become as relaxed as possible when going into the examination room. The test-taker will also have time to eat well and eat sensibly. Know that the brain needs food as much as the rest of the body. With enough food and enough sleep, as well as a relaxed attitude, the body and the mind are primed for success.

Avoid any anxious classmates who are talking about the exam. These students only spread anxiety, and are not worth sharing the anxious sentimentalities.

Before the test also involves creating a positive attitude, so mental preparation should also be a point of concentration. There are many keys to creating a positive attitude. Should fears become rushing in, make a visualization of taking the exam, doing well, and seeing an A written on the paper. Write out a list of affirmations that will bring a feeling of confidence, such as "I am doing well in my English class," "I studied well and know my material," "I enjoy this class." Even if the affirmations aren't believed at first, it sends a positive message to the subconscious which will result in an alteration of the overall belief system, which is the system that creates reality.

If a sensation of panic begins, work with the fear and imagine the very worst! Work through the entire scenario of not passing the test, failing the entire course, and dropping out of school, followed by not getting a job, and pushing a shopping cart through the dark alley where you'll live. This will place things into perspective! Then, practice deep breathing and create a visualization of the opposite situation - achieving an "A" on the exam, passing the entire course, receiving the degree at a graduation ceremony.

On the day of the test, there are many things to be done to ensure the best results, as well as the most calm outlook. The following stages are suggested in order to maximize test-taking potential:

Begin the examination day with a moderate breakfast, and avoid any coffee or beverages with caffeine if the test taker is prone to jitters. Even people who are used to managing caffeine can feel jittery or light-headed when it is taken on a test day.
Attempt to do something that is relaxing before the examination begins. As last minute cramming clouds the mastering of overall concepts, it is better to use this time to create a calming outlook.
Be certain to arrive at the test location well in advance, in order to provide time to select a location that is away from doors, windows and other distractions, as well as giving enough time to relax before the test begins.
Keep away from anxiety generating classmates who will upset the sensation of stability and relaxation that is being attempted before the exam.
Should the waiting period before the exam begins cause anxiety, create a self-distraction by reading a light magazine or something else that is relaxing and simple.

During the exam itself, read the entire exam from beginning to end, and find out how much time should be allotted to each individual problem. Once writing the exam, should more time be taken for a problem, it should be abandoned, in order to begin another problem. If there is time at the end, the unfinished problem can always be returned to and completed.

Read the instructions very carefully - twice - so that unpleasant surprises won't follow during or after the exam has ended.

When writing the exam, pretend that the situation is actually simply the completion of homework within a library, or at home. This will assist in forming a relaxed atmosphere, and will allow the brain extra focus for the complex thinking function.

Begin the exam with all of the questions with which the most confidence is felt. This will build the confidence level regarding the entire exam and will begin a quality momentum. This will also create encouragement for trying the problems where uncertainty resides.

Going with the "gut instinct" is always the way to go when solving a problem. Second guessing should be avoided at all costs. Have confidence in the ability to do well.

For essay questions, create an outline in advance that will keep the mind organized and make certain that all of the points are remembered. For multiple choice, read every answer, even if the correct one has been spotted - a better one may exist.

Continue at a pace that is reasonable and not rushed, in order to be able to work carefully. Provide enough time to go over the answers at the end, to check for small errors that can be corrected.

Should a feeling of panic begin, breathe deeply, and think of the feeling of the body releasing sand through its pores. Visualize a calm, peaceful place, and include all of the sights, sounds and sensations of this image. Continue the deep breathing, and take a few minutes to continue this with closed eyes. When all is well again, return to the test.

If a "blanking" occurs for a certain question, skip it and move on to the next question. There will be time to return to the other question later. Get everything done that can be done, first, to guarantee all the grades that can be compiled, and to build all of the confidence possible. Then return to the weaker questions to build the marks from there.

Remember, one's own reality can be created, so as long as the belief is there, success will follow. And remember: anxiety can happen later, right now, there's an exam to be written!

After the examination is complete, whether there is a feeling for a good grade or a bad grade, don't dwell on the exam, and be certain to follow through on the reward that was promised...and enjoy it! Don't dwell on any mistakes that have been made, as there is nothing that can be done at this point anyway.

Additionally, don't begin to study for the next test right away. Do something relaxing for a while, and let the mind relax and prepare itself to begin absorbing information again.

From the results of the exam - both the grade and the entire experience, be certain to learn from what has gone on. Perfect studying habits and work some more on confidence in order to make the next examination experience even better than the last one.

Learn to avoid places where openings occurred for laziness, procrastination and day dreaming.

Use the time between this exam and the next one to better learn to relax, even learning to relax on cue, so that any anxiety can be controlled during the next exam. Learn how to relax the body. Slouch in your chair if that helps. Tighten and then relax all of the different muscle groups, one group at a time, beginning with the feet and then working all the way up to the neck and face. This will ultimately relax the muscles more than they were to begin with. Learn how to breathe deeply and comfortably, and focus on this breathing going in and out as a relaxing thought. With every exhale, repeat the word "relax."

As common as test anxiety is, it is very possible to overcome it. Make yourself one of the test-takers who overcome this frustrating hindrance.

Additional Bonus Material

Due to our efforts to try to keep this book to a manageable length, we've created a link that will give you access to all of your additional bonus material.

Please visit http://www.mometrix.com/bonus948/cgfm2gafrb to access the information.